The Gospel of
MATTHEW

THE MORNINGSTAR VISION BIBLE

by Rick Joyner

The Gospel of Matthew, The MorningStar Vision Bible
by Rick Joyner
Copyright © 2013
Trade Size Edition

Distributed by MorningStar Publications, Inc.,
a division of MorningStar Fellowship Church
375 Star Light Drive, Fort Mill, SC 29715
www.MorningStarMinistries.org
1-800-542-0278

International Standard Book Number— 978-1-60708-455-6; 1-60708-455-4

Cover Design: Kevin Lepp
Book Layout: Kevin Lepp

For a free catalog of MorningStar Resources,
please call 1-800-542-0278.

The Gospel of Matthew
TABLE OF CONTENTS

PREFACE
THE MORNINGSTAR VISION BIBLE
BY RICK JOYNER

Next to His Son and the Holy Spirit, the Bible is God's greatest gift to mankind. What treasure on earth could be compared to one Word from God? There is good reason why the Bible is the bestselling book of all-time by such a wide margin. The importance of the Bible cannot be overstated. If Jesus, who is the Word, would take His stand on the written Word when challenged by the devil, how much more must we be established on that Word to take our stand and live our lives by it?

The most basic purpose of **The MorningStar Vision Bible** is accuracy and faithfulness to the intended meaning of the Author, the Holy Spirit. His written Word reveals the path to life, salvation, transformation, deliverance, and healing for every soul who would seek to know God. The universe is upheld by the Word of His power, so there is no stronger foundation that we could ever build our lives on other than His Word. Therefore, we have pursued this project with the utmost care in that what is presented here is His Word and not ours. We were very careful not to let anyone work on it that had an agenda other than a love for the truth and the deepest respect for the fact that we were handling this most precious treasure—God's own Word.

The primary accuracy of any translation is its adherence to the original text in the original languages the Bible was written in, Hebrew and Greek. However, there are problems when you try to translate from a language such as Greek into a language like English because Greek is so much more expressive than English. For example, there are several different Greek words with different meanings that are translated as one word "love" in our English version. The Greek words distinguish between such things as friendship love, erotic attraction, or unconditional love. When we just translate these as "love," then it may be generally true, but something basic in what the Author tried to convey is left out. As we mature in Christ by following the Spirit, these deeper, more specific meanings become important. Therefore, we have sought to include the nuances of the Greek language in this version.

A basic biblical guide we used for this work was Psalm 12:6-7: **"The words of the Lord are pure words; as silver tried in a furnace on the earth, refined seven times."** Every Book we release of this version has been through a meticulous process to ensure faithfulness to the original intent at least seven times. Even so, we do not consider this yet to be a completed work. We are releasing these Book by Book in softcover to seek even further examination by those who read it. We are asking our readers to send us challenges for any word, phrase, or part that you think may not be accurate, along with your reasons. These will be received, considered, and researched with openness. If you have insights that you think should be added to the commentary, we will consider those as well.

You can email these or any comments that you have to bible@ morningstarministries.org, or mail them to us at:

MorningStar Publications
375 Star Light Drive
Fort Mill, South Carolina 29715

Please include any credentials that you might have that would be relevant, but they are not necessary for this.

My personal credentials for compiling and editing such a work are first my love for the Bible and my respect for its integrity. I have been a Christian for more than forty years, and I have read the Bible through from cover-to-cover at least once a year. I do have an earned doctorate in theology from a good, accredited school, but have not used the title because I want my message received on the merits of its content, not by a title. Though I have been in pursuit of knowing the Lord and His Word for more than forty years, I still feel more comfortable thinking of myself as a student rather than an expert. If that bothers you I understand, but when handling the greatest truth the world has ever known, I feel we must be as humble and transparent as possible.

Most of those who have worked on this project with me have been students at MorningStar University. This is a unique school that has had students from ages sixteen to over eighty years old. Some have been remarkably skilled in languages, especially Hebrew and Greek. Some have been believers and students of the Word for a long time. Others were fairly new to the faith, but were strong and devoted to seeking and knowing the truth. These were the ones that I was especially interested in recruiting for this project because of the Lord's statement in Matthew 11:25:

> **At that time Jesus answered and said, "I praise You, O Father, Lord of heaven and earth, that You did hide these things from the wise and intelligent and did reveal them to babes."**

Because **"God resists the proud, but gives grace to the humble" (see James 4:6; I Peter 5:5 NKJV)**, the humility of a relatively young believer can be more important for discerning truth than great knowledge and experience if these have caused us to become proud.

Also, as Peter stated concerning Paul's writings in II Peter 3:15-16:

> **Paul, according to the wisdom given him, wrote to you,**
>
> **as also in all his letters, speaking in them of these things, in which are some things hard to**

understand, which the untaught and unstable distort, as they do also the rest of the Scriptures, to their own destruction.

So the untaught can be prone to distort the truth if they are also unstable. This is why the relatively young believers that I sought to be a part of our team were not just stable but strong in the Lord and their resolve to know the truth.

Even so, not everyone who has great knowledge and experience has become so proud that it causes God to resist them. Those who have matured and yet remained humble and teachable are some of the greatest treasures we may have in the body of Christ. Such elders are certainly worthy of great honor and should be listened to and heeded. Nowhere in Scripture are we exhorted to honor the youth, but over and over we are commanded to honor the elders.

So it seems we have a paradox—the Lord reveals His ways to babes, but elders are the ones responsible for keeping His people on the path of life walking in His ways. This is not a contradiction. As with many of the paradoxes in Scripture, the tension between the extremes is intended to help keep us on the path of life by giving us boundaries. Pride in our experience and knowledge can cause us to stray from this path, as can our lack of knowledge if it is combined with instability. The vision and exuberance of youth are needed to keep the fire of passion for the Lord and His ways burning. This is why the Lord said that the wise brought forth from their treasures things both new and old (see Matthew 13:52).

For this reason, I sought the young in the faith who are also stable and displayed a discipline and devotion to obedience to the truth. I also sought the contributions of the experienced and learned who continued to have the humility to whom God gives His grace. As far as Greek and Hebrew scholars, I was more interested in those who are technically-minded, devoted to details, and who seemed to be free of doctrinal prejudices.

This is not to give the impression that all who worked on this project went over the entire Bible. I did have some who went over the entire New Testament, but most only worked on a single Book, and sometimes just a single issue. I may not have told many of the Greek and Hebrew experts that it was for this project when I inquired about a matter with them.

I realize that this is a unique way to develop a Bible version, but as we are told in I Corinthians 13:12 we "see in part" and **"know in part."** Therefore, we all need to put what we have together with what others have if we are going to have a complete picture. This version is the result of many years of labor by many people. Having been a publisher for many years, I know every editor or proofreader will tend to catch different things, and so it has been with this project. We also realize that as hard as we have worked on being as accurate as possible, we may have missed some things, and we will be genuinely appreciative of every one that is caught by our readers. Again, our goal is to have the most accurate English version of the Bible possible.

Even though accuracy and faithfulness to the original intent of the Holy Spirit were our most basic devotions, we also sought insights that could come from many other factors, such as the culture of the times in which the different Books of the Bible were written. Along with myself, many other contributors have spent countless hours of research examining words, phrases, the authors of the Books of the Bible, their times, and even the history of cities and places mentioned in it. Though the knowledge gained by this research did not affect the words in the text of the Bible, they sometimes gave a greater illumination and depth to their meaning that was profound. Sometimes they made obscure, hard to comprehend phrases come to life.

One of the obvious intents of the Author was to be able to communicate to any seeker of truth on the level they are on. For the most basic seeker, knowing such things as the nuances or more detailed meaning of the Greek or Hebrew words may not be important. As we mature, we will seek deeper understanding if we follow the Holy Spirit. We are told in I Corinthians 2:10, **"For to us God revealed them through the Spirit; for the Spirit searches all things, even the depths of God."** Therefore, those who follow the Spirit will not be shallow in their understanding of anything and will especially search to know the depths of the nature of God.

Our single greatest hope is that **The MorningStar Vision Bible** will accurately reveal the will and intent of the Lord, and compel all who read it to love Him more, which is the chief purpose of man. If we love Him more, we will then begin to love one another more. As we grow in love, we will also grow in our devotion to know Him even more, know His ways, and do the things that please Him. He deserves this from us more than could ever be expressed.

There is nothing greater than knowing Him. I am convinced that anything we learn about God will make us love Him more, which is our chief purpose and the one thing that will determine if we are successful human beings. This is also the only thing that can lead to the true peace and true joy that is beyond anything this world can supply. There is no greater adventure that can be had in this life than the true Christian life. The Bible is the map to the greatest quest and the greatest adventure that we could ever experience.

INTRODUCTION
THE GOSPEL OF MATTHEW
BY RICK JOYNER AND CHRIS WHIDDON

The Gospel of Matthew is a history that spans the lineage, birth, life, death, and resurrection of Jesus Christ. It is the longest of the Gospels. Written around 60 A.D. by Matthew, who was one of the twelve original apostles, this Gospel begins by listing the lineage of Jesus Christ starting with Abraham, establishing that Jesus is a prophesied "Son of David," one of the basic qualifications for Him to be the Messiah.

Then Matthew relates how Jesus fulfills the other Messianic prophecies, establishing with overwhelming scriptural proof that He is indeed the promised Messiah. No other person has ever had such credentials. The birth, life, death, and resurrection of Jesus were all prophesied with remarkable detail and accuracy by many prophets dating back many centuries. Such foretelling of the life and purpose of a person like this is unique in human history, making the most solid foundation to build our faith upon that Jesus is indeed the promised Savior. Because this Gospel of Matthew references so many of these prophecies and explains how they were fulfilled, it is considered to be the foundational Gospel.

The detailed accounts of the life of Jesus in this Gospel are also events that are well corroborated by other historical accounts such as the history written by Josephus. This is why Matthew's Gospel was made the first Book of the New Testament and to set a high standard of documentation and verification for the

New Testament. Because all but eleven verses of the entire New Testament are referenced by the writings of the early church fathers, who were the direct disciples of the original twelve apostles, the New Testament is the most scientifically verified Book in the world.

After the parents of Jesus, Mary and Joseph, settle in the town of Nazareth, the account jumps ahead nearly thirty years, introducing John the Baptist and his ministry to prepare Israel for their Messiah. When Jesus was baptized by John, the Holy Spirit came upon Him and remained. Then the Father Himself introduced Jesus as His Son with an audible voice from heaven. He was the One Israel had been waiting for since Moses had first told the young nation that one day a Prophet would come whose life foreshadowed his own life, and this was the One they must follow.

After His baptism, Jesus was led by the Spirit into the desert to be tempted by Satan. When He had completed a 40-day fast and resisted the temptations of Satan, Jesus began His mission in the power of the Holy Spirit. He went about teaching and preaching while healing those who were sick, casting out demons, and astonishing the people throughout the land who had never seen or heard of such works before.

After selecting twelve disciples who would be His closest friends, students, as well as heirs of His authority on the earth, Jesus traveled throughout Israel proclaiming the gospel of the kingdom. While doing this, He performed miracles that demonstrated the authority of the kingdom over the conditions and problems of mankind on the earth. After the disciples witnessed the works of the Holy Spirit, Jesus commissioned them to **"heal the sick, raise the dead, cleanse the lepers, cast out demons" (see Matthew 10:8)** in His name, and they did it. They are still doing it today.

Near the end of Jesus' ministry, He began to tell His disciples that He would be betrayed into the hands of men, suffer torture, and then die, but would be raised on the third day after His death. Just as Jesus predicted, He was betrayed by Judas Iscariot and arrested, interrogated, tortured, and crucified. Matthew gives a short testimony to Jesus' resurrection and includes the resurrected Jesus' last words as He gives the apostles the assurance that He would be with them **"to the end of the age"** (see Matthew 28:20). He does remain with His people, and the Gospels tell us how, because as the Scriptures make clear, He is the same today that He was yesterday—He never changes. This is the ultimate proof of this testimony—He continues to do His works through His people.

THE GOSPEL OF
MATTHEW
Matthew 1

Genealogy of the Messiah

1 The book of the generation of Jesus Christ, the son of David, the son of Abraham.

2 Abraham begot Isaac, Isaac begot Jacob, and Jacob begot Judah and his brothers.

3 Judah begot Perez and Zerah by Tamar. Perez begot Hezron, and Hezron begot Ram.

4 Ram begot Amminadab, Amminadab begot Nahshon, and Nahshon begot Salmon.

5 Salmon begot Boaz by Rahab. Boaz begot Obed by Ruth. Obed begot Jesse,

6 and Jesse begot David the king. David begot Solomon by the one who had been the wife of Uriah.

7 Solomon begot Rehoboam, Rehoboam begot Abijah, and Abijah begot Asa.

8 Asa begot Jehoshaphat, Jehoshaphat begot Joram, and Joram begot Uzziah.

9 Uzziah begot Jotham, Jotham begot Ahaz, and Ahaz begot Hezekiah.

10 Hezekiah begot Manasseh, Manasseh begot Amon, and Amon begot Josiah.

11 Josiah begot Jeconiah and his brothers about the time they were carried away to Babylon.

12 And after they were brought to Babylon, Jeconiah begot Shealtiel, and Shealtiel begot Zerubbabel.

13 Zerubbabel begot Abiud, Abiud begot Eliakim, and Eliakim begot Azor.

14 Azor begot Zadok, Zadok begot Achim, and Achim begot Eliud.

15 Eliud begot Eleazar, Eleazar begot Matthan, and Matthan begot Jacob.

16 Jacob begot Joseph the husband of Mary, to whom was born Jesus who is the Christ.

17 So there are fourteen generations from Abraham to David; fourteen generations from David until the carrying away into Babylon, and fourteen generations from the carrying away into Babylon until Christ.

Birth of the Messiah

18 Now the birth of Jesus Christ happened in this way: When His mother Mary was engaged to be married to Joseph, before they came together, she was found to be with child by the Holy Spirit.

19 Then Joseph her husband, being a just man, and not willing to make her a public example, determined to keep the matter private while breaking off the engagement.

20 While he was considering how to do this, the angel of the Lord appeared to him in a dream, saying, "Joseph, you are a son of David. Do not be afraid to take Mary as your wife, for that which is conceived in her is by the Holy Spirit.

21 "She will have a Son, and you shall call His name Jesus, because He will save His people from their sin."

22 Now all this came about that it might be fulfilled which was spoken by the Lord through the prophet, saying,

23 **"Behold, a virgin shall be with child, and shall bring forth a son, and they shall call his name Emmanuel, which being interpreted means, 'God with us'"** (Isaiah 7:14).

24 After Joseph awakened he did just as the angel of the Lord had instructed him to do and took her as his wife.

25 Neither did he have relations with her until she gave birth to her firstborn son, and he called His name Jesus.

Genealogy of the Messiah

Matthew 1:1-17: The genealogy of Jesus is important because He was prophesied to be from the Tribe of Judah and a descendent of David.

Birth of the Messiah

1:18-25: To be the Savior, Jesus had to be both God and man. Salvation was beyond man's ability and could only come from above. This is why Jesus had to be born of the seed of the Holy Spirit. He also had to be man to make the atonement sacrifice for the sin of man, which is why Jesus most often referred to Himself as "the Son of Man." The earth had been given to man to rule over, and only a man could redeem it.

The extraordinary obedience of both Mary and Joseph was crucial for the coming of the Savior, as well as all of the works of God. It was disobedience that made the atonement necessary, and a foundation of obedience is necessary for the redemption of man. Obedience begins to bring us back under the domain of God. When we obey Him as we should, then the domain that He gave to us will begin to obey us as it should. This is a process of redemption, reconciliation, and then restoration that is the most basic theme of the Scriptures.

NOTES

THE GOSPEL OF
MATTHEW
Matthew 2

The Wise Men

1 Now when Jesus was born in Bethlehem of Judea, in the days of Herod the king, wise men came from the east to Jerusalem, saying,

2 Saying, "Where is He that is born King of the Jews? We have seen His star in the east and have come to worship Him."

3 When Herod the king heard about this, he was troubled, and all of Jerusalem with him.

4 Then he gathered the chief priests and scribes of the people together, and he demanded from them information about where the Christ would be born.

5 They said to him, "In Bethlehem of Judea, because it is what is written by the prophet,

6 'And you, Bethlehem, in the land of Judah, you are not the least among the princes of Judah: for out of you shall come a Ruler who shall shepherd My people Israel'" (Micah 5:2).

7 Then Herod secretly called the wise men and inquired of them urgently about when the star appeared.

8 Then he sent them to Bethlehem and said, "Go and search diligently for the young child, and when you have found Him, bring back word to me that I may come and worship Him also."

9 When they had listened to the king they departed, and the star that they had seen in the east went before them until it came and stood over the place where the young child was.

10 When they saw the star, they rejoiced greatly.

11 When they came into the house, they saw the young child with Mary His mother, and they fell down and worshiped Him. Then they opened their treasures and presented gifts to Him of gold, frankincense, and myrrh.

12 After being warned by God in a dream that they should not return to Herod, they departed for their own country a different way.

13 After they had departed, the angel of the Lord appeared to Joseph in a dream, saying, "Arise, and take the young child and his mother and flee into Egypt. Stay there until I bring you word, because Herod will seek to destroy the young child."

Sojourn in Egypt

14 When he awakened, he took the young child and His mother while it was still dark and departed for Egypt.

15 They remained there until the death of Herod so that it might be fulfilled which was spoken of the Lord by the prophet, saying, "Out of Egypt have I called My Son" (Hosea 11:1).

16 When Herod saw that he had been fooled by the wise men, he began raging and gave orders to slay all of the children that were in Bethlehem and in all the coasts around it, from two years old and under, according to the time which he had ascertained from the wise men that the child should be born.

17 In this way, it was fulfilled that which was spoken by Jeremiah the prophet, saying,

18 "In Rama there was heard, lamentation, weeping, and great mourning, Rachel weeping for her children, and could not be comforted because they were no more" (Jeremiah 31:15).

19 When Herod was dead, an angel of the Lord appeared in a dream to Joseph while he was in Egypt, saying,

20 "Arise, and take the young child and His mother, and go into the land of Israel, as those who sought the child's life are dead."

21 So he arose, and took the young child and His mother, and came to the land of Israel.

22 When he heard that Archelaus reigned in Judea in the place of his father Herod, he was afraid to go there, and being warned by God in a dream, he turned and went to the region of Galilee:

23 So he found a place to stay in a city called Nazareth, so that it might be fulfilled which was spoken by the prophets, "He shall be called a Nazarene" (Isaiah 11:1).

The Wise Men

Matthew 2:1-13: The only way that one could find the Messiah was by revelation from above. This is still true. "Wise men still seek Him," and those who seek are promised that they will find Him. There is no greater wisdom on this earth than to seek the Lord. There is no greater promise that has been given than if we seek Him, we will find Him.

The way that these wise men worshiped Jesus was to bring Him gifts. This is still wisdom. The Lord is practical, and these gifts obviously sustained Him and His family while they sojourned in Egypt to escape the evil intentions of Herod.

Sojourn in Egypt

2:14-23: The condition of the world is such that the Son of God could be born among men and His life would be threatened from beginning to end. It's not any better, and anything that is truly born of God must live in this world under continual threat and attack. This is also the test in this age by which it is determined who is worthy to rule in the age to come as a joint heir with Him.

When Moses prophesied of the coming Savior, he had said that the Lord would raise up a prophet like him. In many ways, the life of Moses did parallel the life of Jesus who was also coming to set God's people free. When both were born, there was an attempt to destroy them by killing Hebrew infants. Like Moses and Jesus, the prophets also speak of a great host in the last days which will bring great deliverance to many. In this same way, the devil seeks to destroy them through abortion, drugs, and lawlessness. Even so, through the most trying times, they will have been tried and found true.

It is noteworthy that the Lord guided the parents of Jesus by dreams. This is one of the primary ways that He has spoken

to and given guidance to His people from the beginning, and as we see in places like Acts 2:17-18, it will be until the end of this age.

NOTES

THE GOSPEL OF
MATTHEW
Matthew 3

John the Baptist

1 In those days John the Baptist came preaching in the wilderness of Judea, saying,

2 "Repent! The kingdom of heaven is at hand."

3 For this is the one that was spoken of by the prophet Isaiah, saying, "The voice of one crying in the wilderness, 'Prepare the way of the Lord, and make his way straight'" (Isaiah 40:3).

4 John's clothing was made of camel's hair, and he had a leather girdle about his loins; and his food was locusts and wild honey.

5 Then all of Jerusalem, and all of Judea, and all of the region around the Jordan River, went out to hear him,

6 and they were baptized by him in Jordan, confessing their sins.

7 When he saw many of the Pharisees and Sadducees come to be baptized, he said to them, "O generation of vipers, who has warned you to flee from the wrath to come?

8 "Bring forth fruit that proves you have repented.

9 "Do not think within yourselves, 'We have Abraham as our father:' I say to you that God is able to raise up children of Abraham from these stones.

10 "Now the axe is being laid to the root of the trees. Therefore, every tree that does not bring forth good fruit will be cut down and cast into the fire.

11 "I indeed baptize you with water for repentance, but He that is coming after me is greater than I am. I am not even worthy to tie

His sandals. He is the One who will baptize you with the Holy Spirit and with fire.

12 "His fan is in His hand, and He will thoroughly purge His floor and gather His wheat into the barn; but He will burn up the chaff with unquenchable fire."

Jesus' Baptism

13 Then Jesus came from Galilee to the Jordan to be baptized by John.

14 But John resisted Him, saying, "I need to be baptized by You! Why do You come to me?"

15 Jesus answered him, "You must allow it. It must be done to fulfill all righteousness." Then he baptized Him.

16 When Jesus was baptized, as soon as He came up out of the water, the heavens were opened to Him, and He saw the Spirit of God descending like a dove and remaining upon Him.

17 Then a voice from heaven said, "This is My beloved Son, in whom I am well pleased."

John the Baptist

Matthew 3:1-12: John the Baptist's call to repentance was not because judgment was coming, but because the kingdom was at hand. Yet his description of the coming Messiah that he was preparing the way for was quite severe—He would cut down the trees that were not bearing fruit and burn the chaff with fire. We must never forget the love with which He loved us to come and make atonement for us, but neither should we forget that He is also severe in righteousness. This is why Paul wrote in Romans 11:22 that we must "behold now the kindness and the severity of God." If we cannot see both together, we cannot see Him as He is.

Jesus' Baptism

3:13-17: John was the representative of all who had prepared the way for the Lord. They were the Old Order, under

the Old Covenant, but Jesus honored them by submitting to John's baptism. A core value of all who would serve the Lord is to honor their fathers and mothers, both natural and spiritual. One way that we do this is to be immersed, or baptized, in their teachings.

The Holy Spirit alighted on many before Jesus, using them and empowering them to do God's work, but Jesus was the first that the Holy Spirit came upon and remained. He was the tabernacle, the habitation of God, not just a worker.

NOTES

THE GOSPEL OF
MATTHEW
Matthew 4

The Temptation of Christ

1 Then the Spirit led Jesus into the wilderness to be tempted by the devil.

2 After He had fasted for forty days and forty nights, He was hungry.

3 Then the tempter came to Him, he said, "If You are the Son of God, command these stones to be turned into bread."

4 He answered and said, **"It is written, 'Man shall not live by bread alone, but by every word that proceeds from the mouth of God'" (Deuteronomy 8:3).**

5 Then the devil took Him up into the holy city and set Him on a pinnacle of the temple,

6 There he said to Him, **"If you are the Son of God, jump off. For it is written, 'He shall give his angels charge concerning you, and they hold you up so that you will not dash your foot against a stone'"** (Psalm 91:11).

7 Jesus said to him, "It is written again, **'You shall not tempt the Lord your God'"** (Deuteronomy 6:16).

8 Again, the devil took Him up into a very high mountain, and showed Him all the kingdoms of the world and the glory of them,

9 and said to Him, "All these things I will give to You, if You will fall down and worship me."

10 Then Jesus said to him, "Depart from here, Satan! It is written, **'You shall worship the Lord your God, and Him only shall you serve'"** (Deuteronomy 6:13).

11 Then the devil left Him, and angels came and ministered to Him.

12 Now when Jesus heard that John had been cast into prison, He departed for Galilee.

13 Leaving Nazareth, He came and dwelt in Capernaum, which is on the sea coast, in the borders of Zebulun and Naphtali.

14 This fulfilled what was spoken by Isaiah the prophet, saying,

15 **"The land of Zebulun and the land of Naphtali, by the way of the sea, beyond Jordan, Galilee of the Gentiles—**

16 **"The people who sat in darkness saw great light; and to those who dwelt in the shadow of death light sprang forth"** (Isaiah 9:1-2).

17 From that time Jesus began to preach, saying, "Repent: for the kingdom of heaven is at hand."

Calling the Disciples

18 As Jesus was walking by the Sea of Galilee, He saw two brothers, Simon who is called Peter, and Andrew his brother, casting a net into the sea, because they were fishermen.

19 So He said to them, "Follow Me, and I will make you fishers of men."

20 They immediately left their nets and followed Him.

21 Going on from there, He saw two more brothers, James the son of Zebedee, and John his brother, who were in a ship with Zebedee their father mending their nets, and He called them.

22 They immediately left the ship, and their father, and followed Him.

23 Jesus then went about the land of Galilee, teaching in their synagogues, and preaching the gospel of the kingdom, and healing every kind of sickness and disease among the people.

24 His fame went throughout all Syria; and they brought to Him all sick people that were taken with all kinds of diseases and torments. Those who were possessed with devils, and those who were mentally ill, and those that had the palsy, and He healed them.

25 So great multitudes followed Him from Galilee, Decapolis, and from Jerusalem, and all around Judea, even from beyond Jordan.

The Temptation of Christ

Matthew 4:1-16: Immediately after the Holy Spirit comes upon Him, Jesus did not go seek the crowds, but He went into the wilderness to fast and pray. Fasting is a spiritual discipline of denying and humbling ourselves before God seeking His grace. If the Son of God had to do this, how much more do we?

There are different ways to fast. One is not eating food, or certain foods, and another can be denying ourselves certain activities, such as watching television, or just the news, or sports, etc. However, when we do this, the Lord does seem to always honor it. Virtually all of the great healing and miracle ministries began with a forty-day fast from food. The Lord promises that if we will seek Him we will find Him, and this kind of earnest seeking has been a major way that He has been found in both the Scriptures and history.

After fasting, Jesus, while in a weakened, hungry state, was tempted by the devil. To thwart the devil's temptations, Jesus, who is the Word, took His stand on the written Word. If the Son of God had to do this, how much more do we?

Calling the Disciples

4:17-25: After fasting, praying, and resisting the temptations of the devil, Jesus set about to do what He was called to do—preach the gospel of the kingdom, heal the sick, and set the captives free. This is also the work that He gave His disciples to do until He returns.

NOTES

THE GOSPEL OF
MATTHEW
Matthew 5

The Sermon on the Mount

1 Seeing the multitudes, He went up into a mountain. After He had sat down, His disciples came to Him.

2 He then began to teach them, saying,

3 "Blessed are the poor in spirit, for theirs is the kingdom of heaven.

4 "Blessed are those who mourn, for they will be comforted.

5 "Blessed are the meek, for they will inherit the earth.

6 "Blessed are those who hunger and thirst for righteousness, for they will be filled.

7 "Blessed are the merciful, for they will obtain mercy.

8 "Blessed are the pure in heart, for they will see God.

9 "Blessed are the peacemakers, for they will be called the children of God.

10 "Blessed are those who are persecuted for righteousness' sake, for theirs is the kingdom of heaven.

11 "Blessed are you when men revile you and persecute you, and say all manner of evil about you falsely for My sake.

12 "Rejoice when this happens, and be exceedingly glad, because great is your reward in heaven, and it was in this same way that they persecuted the prophets who came before you.

13 "You are the salt of the earth, but if the salt has lost its savor how will it become salty again? It is then good for nothing, except to be cast out and to be trodden under foot by men.

14 "You are the light of the world. A city that is set on a hill cannot be hidden.

15 "Neither do men light a candle and then put it under a bushel basket. They put it on a candlestick so that it gives light to all that are in the house.

16 "Let your light so shine before men so that they may see your good works, and by them glorify your Father who is in heaven.

The Law and Righteousness

17 "Do not think that I have come to destroy the law, or the prophets. I have not come to destroy it, but to fulfill it.

18 "It is true that until heaven and earth passes away not a single letter or stroke will pass away from the law until all of it has been fulfilled.

19 "Whoever therefore will break one of the least commandments, and teach others to do so, he will be called the least in the kingdom of heaven. Whoever will both do and teach them, the same will be called great in the kingdom of heaven.

20 "For I say to you, except your righteousness exceeds the righteousness of the scribes and Pharisees, you will in no way enter the kingdom of heaven.

21 "You have heard that it was said, **'You shall not kill'** (Exodus 20:13; Deuteronomy 5:17, 16:18)**,** and whoever kills will face the judgment.

22 "I say to you, whoever is angry with his brother without a cause will be in danger of the judgment. Whoever says to his brother, 'You worthless one,' will be in danger of judgment before the court, but whoever will say, 'You fool,' will be in danger of being cast into Gehenna.

23 "Therefore, if you bring your gift to the altar, and there you remember that your brother has something against you;

24 "leave your gift at the altar, and go be reconciled to your brother, and then come and offer your gift.

25 "Agree with your adversary quickly while you are on the way to court with him, so that your adversary does not deliver you to the judge, and the judge deliver you to the warden, and you are thrown into prison.

26 "Truly I say to you, you will not come out of there until you have paid the last cent.

27 "You have heard that it was said originally, **'You shall not commit adultery'** (Exodus 20:14; Deuteronomy 5:18).

28 "I say to you that whoever looks at a woman to lust after her has committed adultery with her already in his heart.

29 "If your right eye causes you to stumble, pluck it out, and cast it away. It is better for you to lose one part of your body than for your whole body to be cast into Gehenna.

30 "If your right hand causes you to stumble, cut if off, and cast it away. It is better for you to lose one part of your body than to have your whole body cast into Gehenna.

31 "It has been said, 'Whoever will put away his wife, let him give her a certificate of divorce,

32 "but I say to you that whoever will put away his wife, except for the cause of immorality, causes her to commit adultery, and whoever marries one who is put away commits adultery.

33 "Again, you have heard that it has been said originally, **'You will not swear falsely, and you shall perform the promises that you make to the Lord'** (Ecclesiastes 5:4).

34 "But I say to you, do not swear at all, neither by heaven, because it is God's throne,

35 "nor by the earth, because it is His footstool, neither by Jerusalem; for it is the city of the great King.

36 "Neither should you swear by your own head, because you cannot make one hair white or black.

37 "Let your 'Yes' mean 'Yes' and your 'No' mean 'No.' Anything but this is evil.

38 "You have heard that it has been said, **'An eye for an eye, and a tooth for a tooth.'** (Exodus 21:24; Leviticus 24:20; Deuteronomy 19:21)

39 "I say to you, do not resist one who seeks to do you evil, but whoever strikes you on the right cheek, turn to him the other also.

40 "If any man sues you to take away your coat, let him have your cloak also.

41 "Whoever would compel you to go a mile, go with him two.

42 "Give to him who asks of you, and do not turn away one who wants to borrow from you.

43 "You have heard that it has been said, **'You shall love your neighbor** (Leviticus 19:18), and 'hate your enemy.'

44 "But I say to you, love your enemies, and bless those who curse you. Do good to those who hate you, and pray for those who despitefully use you, and persecute you.

45 "In this way you prove to be the children of your Father who is in heaven, because He makes His sun to rise on the evil and on the good, and sends rain on the just and the unjust.

46 "For if you love those who love you, what reward do you deserve for that? Don't even the tax collectors do the same?

47 "If you greet only your brothers, what are you doing more than others? Don't even the tax collectors do that?

48 "Therefore you are to be perfect, even as your Father which is in heaven is perfect."

The Sermon on the Mount

Matthew 5:1-16: There are two exceptional contributions that the Gospel of Matthew makes. First, it is strongly devoted to the words and teachings of Jesus, not just His acts, and is the only Gospel to include The Sermon on the Mount. It is also the best for referencing the Old Testament prophecies that Jesus fulfilled or the references to the Old Testament that He used in His teachings.

The most important writings in the Bible, Old or New Testaments, are the teachings of Jesus as recorded in the Gospels. All of the other writings are important and are Scripture, but the teachings of Jesus are the foundation that all of the others stand on. The Sermon on the Mount is an

important part of that foundation and reveals the most basic characteristics that God honors.

The Law and Righteousness

5:17-48: Here Jesus begins to give His interpretation of the Law and Prophets. We can be sure that His interpretation is the correct one. We know by His own words that He did not come to change the Law, to add to it or take away from it, but to fulfill it, so that the ultimate result is that we could walk in the perfect ways of God. We know this can only be achieved by loving God above all things, and loving one another as we should.

NOTES

THE GOSPEL OF
MATTHEW
Matthew 6

Righteous Generosity

1 "Be careful that you do not parade your offerings before men, to be seen by them, otherwise you will have no reward from your Father in heaven.

2 "Therefore, when you present your offerings, do not sound a trumpet as the hypocrites do in the synagogues, or in the streets, so that they may receive recognition from men. Truly, they have their reward.

3 "But when you give offerings, do not let your left hand know what your right hand is doing,

4 "so that your offerings may be a secret between you and the Father. He who sees in secret will Himself reward you openly.

5 "When you pray, do not be like the hypocrites. They love to pray standing in the synagogues and in the corners of the streets, so that they may be seen by men. Truly, they have their reward.

6 "When you pray, enter into your closet, and when you have shut the door, pray to your Father in secret. Then your Father, who sees in secret, shall reward you openly.

7 "When you pray, do not use vain repetitions like the heathen do. They think that they will be heard because of the abundance of words.

8 "Do not be like that. Your Father knows the things you have need of even before you ask Him.

The Lord's Prayer

9 "Pray this way: 'Our Father who is in heaven, holy is Your name.

10 'May Your kingdom come, and Your will be done, on earth as it is in heaven.

11 'Give us this day our daily bread,

12 'and forgive us our trespasses as we forgive those who trespass against us.

13 'Lead us not into temptation, but deliver us from evil, because Yours is the kingdom, and the power, and the glory, forever. Amen.'

Forgiveness and Fasting

14 "For if you forgive men their trespasses, your heavenly Father will also forgive you.

15 "If you do not forgive men their trespasses, neither will your Father forgive your trespasses.

16 "When you fast, do not be as the hypocrites, who wear a sad countenance, and disfigure their faces, so that they may appear to men to be fasting. Truly I say to you, they have their reward.

17 "When you fast, anoint your head, and wash your face,

18 "so that men cannot tell that you are fasting. Then you are doing it for your Father in secret, and your Father who sees in secret shall reward you openly.

True Treasure

19 "Do not store up for yourself treasures upon earth, where moth and rust can corrupt them, and where thieves can break in and steal them.

20 "Lay up for yourselves treasures in heaven, where neither moth nor rust can corrupt, and where thieves cannot break in to steal.

21 "Where your treasure is, there will your heart be also.

22 "The light of the body is the eye. Therefore, if your eye is single, your whole body will be full of light.

23 "If your eye is given to evil, your whole body will be full of darkness. If therefore the light that is in you is darkness, how great is that darkness!

24 "No man can serve two masters, because he will either hate the one and love the other, or he will hold to the one and despise the other. You cannot serve God and the world's riches.

God Will Provide

25 "Therefore I say to you, take no thought for your life, such as what you will eat, or what you will drink, or for the clothes to put on your body. Is not life more than food, and the body more than clothes?

26 "Behold the birds of the air. They do not sow, nor reap, nor do they gather food into barns, yet your heavenly Father feeds them. Are you not worth much more than they are?

27 "Which of you by taking thought can add one cubit to your height?

28 "Why be so concerned about your clothes? Consider the lilies of the field, how they grow. They do not toil, neither do they spin,

29 "and yet I say to you that even Solomon in all of his glory was not arrayed like one of these.

30 "If God so clothes the grass of the field, which is here today but tomorrow is cast into the furnace, will He not much more clothe you, O you of little faith?

31 "Therefore take no thought, saying, 'What will we eat?' or, 'What will we drink?' or, 'With what will we be clothed?'

32 "For your heavenly Father knows that you have need of all these things.

33 "Seek first the kingdom of God, and His righteousness, and all of these things will be given to you.

34 "Therefore, take no thought for tomorrow. Each day has enough cares for itself. Each day has enough problems in it for that day."

Righteous Generosity

Matthew 6:1-8: One of the most important things for a Christian to do is to develop a secret relationship with their Father in heaven, praying in secret and giving in secret. When we do this, we are putting our treasure in heaven, not seeking any gain from human recognition, and where our treasure is there will our heart be. This is one of the primary ways that "the eyes of our hearts," or our spiritual eyes, are opened. What we see with our spiritual eyes should be more real to us than what we see with our natural eyes, because it is.

The Lord's Prayer

6:9-13: Not only should we pray "the Lord's Prayer" regularly out of obedience to the Lord, but we know that the prayer the Son of God gave us to pray will be answered. We know by this that His kingdom will come to the earth, and His will is going to be done on earth just like it is in heaven. This is the greatest hope we can ever have for the earth, and it is a sure hope that will not disappoint.

Forgiveness and Fasting

6:14-18: To be forgiven, we must forgive others. We should have as a main purpose and a lifestyle to take up our crosses daily, which we must do to be His disciples. This means that we should be constantly on the lookout for how we can lay down our own lives and our own self-interests to live for His interests. This begins with forgiving every chance that we can, as the forgiveness of sin is the most basic message of the cross. When we take up the cross to do this, it is also a demonstration of the work of the cross.

Like prayer, fasting is a basic New Covenant discipline. He did not say "if" you fast, but "when" you fast. It is not an option. However, there are many options about how we fast. The Lord who so loves diversity is certainly open to creative fasting. Some may just fast from desserts, others from breads, others from food entirely for a period of time. Some fast from television, or other things that take their time and affections away from the Lord. However we fast, it is a statement of our seriousness with God that He always honors.

True Treasure

6:19-24: When we make our investments in heaven with Him, where our treasure is, there will our hearts be. This one thing can do more than anything else to begin to open the "eyes of our hearts," or our spiritual eyes, and help us to be more spiritually than earthly minded.

6:22: We are told that if our eye is single, we will be full of light. This is the power of a unified vision. Is the main purpose in our life to do His will? Are we seeking first the kingdom and His righteousness? Are we doing all things for the sake of His gospel? This discipline of the disciple, singleness of vision, is the source of the most powerful lives that have ever walked the earth.

God Will Provide

6:25-34: If we have become Christ's slave, then it is the Master's responsibility to take care of the needs of His slaves. If we will put taking care of the Lord's interests above our own, then He will take care of us. There can be no greater deal that we could ever make.

6:33: This is the key to the kingdom, or the key that opens the door to living in the kingdom now.

NOTES

THE GOSPEL OF
MATTHEW
Matthew 7

Unrighteous Judgment

1 "Do not condemn so that you will not be condemned.

2 "For with the same measure of judgment that you give to others, you will be measured by yourself.

3 "So why do you consider the splinter that is in your brother's eye, but do not consider the beam that is in your own eye?

4 "Or will you say to your brother, 'Let me pull out the splinter that is in your eye,' when there is a beam is in your own eye?

5 "You hypocrite! First take out the beam that is in your own eye, and then you can see clearly to take the speck out of your brother's eye.

6 "Do not give what is holy to the dogs, neither cast your pearls before swine, or they will trample them under their feet, and turn and attack you.

Keep Seeking, Asking, Knocking

7 "Keep asking and it will be given to you. Keep seeking and you will find. Keep knocking and it will be opened to you:

8 "For everyone that keeps asking receives, and he who keeps seeking finds, and to the one who keeps knocking it will be opened.

9 "Or what man is there from among you whom, if his son asks for bread, will give him a stone?

10 "Or if he asks for a fish, will he give him a serpent?

11 "If you then, being evil, know how to give good gifts to your

children, how much more will your Father who is in heaven give good things to those who ask Him?

12 "Therefore, whatever you would have others to do for you, you should do for them, because this is the law and the prophets.

The Path of Life

13 "Enter by the narrow gate because the gate is wide, and the way is broad that leads to destruction, and there are many who go that way.

14 "The gate is small, and the way is narrow that leads to life, and few are those who find it.

15 "Beware of false prophets who come to you in sheep's clothing, but inwardly they are ravening wolves.

16 "You will recognize them by their fruit. Do men gather grapes from thorns, or figs of thistles?

17 "Even so, every good tree brings forth good fruit, but a corrupt tree brings forth bad fruit.

18 "A good tree cannot bring forth bad fruit, neither can a corrupt tree bring forth good fruit.

19 "Every tree that does not bring forth good fruit is cut down and cast into the fire.

20 "Therefore by their fruit you will know them.

21 "Not every one who says to Me, 'Lord, Lord,' will enter the kingdom of heaven, but he that does the will of My Father who is in heaven *will enter.*

22 "Many will say to Me in that day, 'Lord, Lord, have we not prophesied in Your name? In Your name did we not cast out devils? In Your name we have done many wonderful works.'

23 "I will declare to them, 'I was never close to you. Depart from Me you who practice lawlessness.'

Building With Wisdom

24 "Therefore whoever hears these words of Mine, and does them, I will liken him to a wise man who built his house upon a rock.

25 "When the rain descended, and the floods came, the winds blew, and beat against that house, but it did not fall because it was built upon a rock.

26 "Every one who hears these words of Mine, and does not do them, will be like a foolish man who built his house upon the sand,

27 "so when the rains came, and then the floods came, and the winds blew, and beat upon that house, great was its fall."

28 When Jesus had finished speaking, the people were astonished at His teaching,

29 because He taught them as one having authority, and not as the scribes do.

Unrighteous Judgment

Matthew 7:1-6: Here we are not being told not to judge others as many suppose, or to not try to get the speck out of a brother's eye, but rather to get the log out of our own first so that we can see well enough to help get the speck out of our brother's eye. The key to not judging wrongly, or hypocritically, is to do it out of sincere love, seeking to help one another, as well as doing it in the humility that would help us see our own problems.

Keep Seeking, Asking, Knocking

7:7-12: It takes "faith and patience" to inherit the promises, so it is persevering prayer that attains.

We must also have faith that what the Lord gives us will always be good, and that all good gifts come from Him. This should result in us always doing that which is good for one another.

The Path of Life

7:13-23: Those who tend to follow the crowds instead of having a close, personal fellowship with the Lord and following Him, almost always will be misled and take the wide path to destruction. To follow the Lord takes the highest level of

integrity and the greatest courage because you will often find yourself going a different way from most others.

The Lord also warns that many would come in His name, declaring that He, Jesus is the Christ, and yet would be deceivers (see Matthew 24:4). For this reason, we do need to examine the fruit of those who claim to be His messengers to see if they are true.

As we see in verses 22-23, many can even do the works of the Lord and have good fruit, but they deceive themselves into thinking that since they have so much good fruit they are right with Him, when they may have drifted far from keeping Him as their first love and loving Him above all things. We must not drift from our highest purpose—to love Him and seek Him, not just to do His works.

Building with Wisdom

7:24-29: It is a great thing to seek to know the teachings of the Lord, but this will not help us unless we obey them and apply them to our lives. As we enter times of increasing volatility and shaking in virtually every area, those who have built their lives on the Rock, knowing His ways and doing them, will become increasingly apparent. If we have not done this, and we too are shaking, then we should do as Paul exhorted in II Corinthians 13:5. We must examine ourselves, measuring our ways by His teachings, and have as a top priority of our life to align ourselves with His teachings.

NOTES

THE GOSPEL OF
MATTHEW
Matthew 8

Jesus Heals the Leper

1 When He had come down from the mountain, great multitudes followed Him.

2 Then a leper came and bowed down to Him, saying, "Lord, if it is Your will, You can make me clean."

3 Jesus stretched out His hand and touched him, saying, "I am willing. Be clean." Immediately his leprosy departed.

4 Then Jesus said to him, "See that you tell no one, but go your way, show yourself to the priest, and offer the gift that Moses commanded as a testimony to them."

The Faith of the Centurion

5 When Jesus entered Capernaum, a centurion came out to meet Him, imploring Him,

6 saying, "Lord, my servant lies at home sick of the palsy and is grievously tormented."

7 Jesus replied to him, "I will come and heal him."

8 The centurion responded, "Lord, I am not worthy for You to come under my roof, but if You just speak the word my servant will be healed.

9 "For I am a man under authority, having soldiers under me, and I say to this man, 'Go,' and he goes, and to another, 'Come,' and he comes, and to my servant, 'Do this,' and he does it."

10 When Jesus heard this He marveled, and said to those who were

following, "Truly, I say to you, I have not found such great faith in Israel.

11 "I say to you that many will come from the east and west, and will sit down with Abraham, Isaac, and Jacob, in the kingdom of heaven.

12 "However, the children of the kingdom will be cast out into outer darkness where there will be weeping and gnashing of teeth."

13 Then Jesus said to the centurion, "Go your way. Just as you have believed it will be done for you." So his servant was healed in the same hour.

14 When Jesus came to Peter's house, He saw his mother-in-law laying down sick with a fever.

15 He touched her hand, and the fever left her, and she arose and served them.

16 When the evening had come, they brought to Him many that were possessed with devils, and He cast out the evil spirits with His word, and healed all that were sick,

17 so that it might be fulfilled that was spoken by Isaiah the prophet, saying, **"He took our infirmities, and bore our sicknesses"** (Isaiah 53:4)

The Cost of Discipleship

18 When Jesus saw the great multitudes around Him, He gave orders for them to depart for the other side.

19 Then a certain scribe came and said to Him, "Master, I will follow You wherever You go."

20 Jesus said to him, "The foxes have holes, and the birds of the air have nests, but the Son of man does not have anywhere to lay his head."

21 Another one of His disciples said to Him, "Lord, please allow me to first go and bury my father."

22 Jesus said to him, "Follow Me, and let the dead bury their dead."

He Calms the Storm

23 When He had entered into a ship, His disciples followed Him aboard.

24 Then a great storm arose while they were at sea, and it was so great that the ship was covered with the waves, but He was sleeping.

25 His disciples came to Him and woke Him, saying, "Lord, save us! We are going to perish!"

26 He said to them, "Why are you afraid, O you of little faith?" Then He arose and rebuked the winds and the sea, and a great calm came upon them.

27 Then the men marveled, saying, "What manner of man is this? Even the winds and the sea obey Him!"

28 When He had come to the other side into the country of the Gadarenes, two men met Him who were possessed with demons. They came out of the tombs and were exceedingly fierce, so that no one would pass by that way.

29 When they beheld the Lord, they cried out, saying, "What have we to do with You, Jesus, Son of God? Have You come here to torment us before the time?"

30 A good distance away there was a large herd of swine feeding.

31 So the devils begged Him, saying, "If You cast us out, send us into the herd of swine."

32 He said to them, "Go!" They immediately came out and entered into the herd of swine, and the whole herd of swine ran violently down a steep bank into the sea, and perished in the waters.

33 The keepers of the swine fled into the city and told everything that had happened to the men who had been possessed by the demons.

34 Then the whole city came out to meet Jesus, and when they saw Him, they begged Him do depart from their region.

Jesus Heals the Leper

Matthew 8:1-4: The testimony of the Gospels is that every person who came to Jesus for healing was healed. This is still true. The key here is to go to Jesus, not just a method or a person. The Lord has given healing gifts to people, and it is right to seek their prayers, but we must see through them to the Spirit of God who is using them.

The Faith of the Centurion

8:5-17: The faith of the centurion was based in his understanding of authority. True faith is simply recognizing who Jesus is and where He sits, above all rule and authority and dominion.

Everywhere the Lord went He healed the sick and cast out demons. This is His nature, to destroy the works of the devil, and to set people free.

The Cost of Discipleship

8:18-22: To be the disciple of the King of kings is the highest purpose anyone can have in this life. To do this half-heartedly would be one of the greatest affronts to God. Those who would be His disciples must give themselves to it without compromise.

He Calms the Storm

8:23-34: Jesus rebuked the storm because it was a demonic storm stirred up by the demons He was to meet on the other side.

NOTES

THE GOSPEL OF
MATTHEW
Matthew 9

The Authority to Forgive Sins

1 He entered into a ship and passed over to His own city.

2 So they brought to Him a man sick with the palsy, lying on a bed. Jesus, seeing their faith, said to the one sick of the palsy, "Son, be of good cheer; your sins have been forgiven."

3 Because of this certain scribes said within themselves, "This man blasphemes."

4 Jesus, knowing their thoughts, said, "Why do you think evil in your hearts?

5 "Is it easier to say, 'Your sins are forgiven,' or to say, 'Arise and walk?'

6 *"I said this* so that you know that the Son of man has power on earth to forgive sins (then He said to the one sick of the palsy), 'Arise, take up your bed, and go to your house.'"

7 So he arose and departed for his house.

8 When the multitudes saw it, they marveled, and glorified God, which had given such power to men.

Calling Sinners to Repentance

9 As Jesus passed from there, He saw a man named Matthew sitting at the customs office, and He said to him, "Follow Me." He arose and followed Him.

10 It came to pass, as Jesus sat down to eat in his house, that many tax collectors and sinners came and sat down with Him and His disciples.

11 When the Pharisees saw it, they said to His disciples, "Why does your Master eat with tax collectors and sinners?"

12 When Jesus heard this He said to them, "They that are well do not need a physician, but rather the ones who are sick.

13 "Go and learn what this means, 'I would rather have mercy than sacrifice.' For I did not come to call the righteous, but sinners to repentance."

Fasting

14 Then the disciples of John came to Him, saying, "Why do we and the Pharisees fast often, but Your disciples do not fast?"

15 Jesus said to them, "Can the children of the bride chamber mourn as long as the bridegroom is with them? Even so, the days will come when the bridegroom will be taken from them, and then shall they fast.

New Wine

16 "No man puts a piece of new cloth on an old garment; for when it shrinks it will pull away from the old cloth so that the tear is made worse.

17 "Neither do men put new wine into old wineskins, or they will burst, and the wine will run out, and the bottles will also be lost. But they put new wine into new bottles, and both are preserved."

18 While He spoke these things to them a certain ruler came and paid homage to Him, then said, "My daughter is now dead, but if You come and lay Your hand on her she shall live."

19 So Jesus arose and followed him, and so did His disciples.

Touching the Hem of His garment

20 A woman who had suffered an issue of blood for twelve years came up behind Him and touched the hem of His garment.

21 She had said within herself, "If I may but touch His garment, I will be made whole."

22 Then Jesus turned around, and when He saw her He said, "Daughter, be comforted. Your faith has made you whole." So the woman was made well from that hour.

Raising the Nobleman's Daughter

23 When Jesus came into the ruler's house, and saw the minstrels and the people making a commotion,

24 He said to them, "Stand back. The maid is not dead, but sleeps." So they scorned Him and laughed.

25 When the people were put out, He went in and took her by the hand, and the maid awakened.

26 The news of this went abroad throughout the land.

Healing the Blind and Dumb

27 As Jesus departed from there, two blind men followed Him, crying out, saying, "Son of David, have mercy on us."

28 When He had come into the house, the blind men came to Him, and Jesus said to them, "Do you believe that I am able to do this?" They said to Him, "Yes, Lord."

29 Then He touched their eyes, saying, "According to your faith let it be it done for you."

30 Their eyes were opened. Then Jesus charged them, saying, "Let no one know about this."

31 When they had departed, they spread His fame throughout the entire region.

32 As they were going out, behold, a dumb man who was demon-possessed was brought to Him.

33 After the demon was cast out, the dumb man spoke, and the multitudes marveled, saying, "Nothing like this was ever seen in Israel."

34 But the Pharisees were saying, "He casts out the demons by the ruler of the demons."

Compassion for the Sheep

35 Jesus then went through all the cities and villages, teaching in their

synagogues, and preaching the gospel of the kingdom, and healing every sickness and every disease among the people.

36 When He saw the multitudes, He was moved with compassion for them, because they were weak and were scattered abroad as sheep without a shepherd.

37 Then He said to His disciples, "The harvest truly is plentiful, but the laborers are few.

38 "Therefore pray to the Lord of the harvest for Him to send more laborers for His harvest."

The Authority to Forgive Sins

Chapter 9:1-8: This one incident illuminates a couple of important factors. The first is that disease can be the result of sin, and forgiveness can heal these diseases. The next was that Jesus was far more prone to forgive than to condemn. He still is.

Calling Sinners to Repentance

9:9-13: Jesus was the most righteous man to ever walk the earth, yet the sinners were attracted to Him. Our righteousness has become a form of legalism if it does not attract the sinners who need grace. How would our service to the Lord change if it were based more in mercy than sacrifice?

Fasting

9:14-15: As the Lord affirms here, fasting would be a basic discipline of His disciples after He departed.

New Wine

9:16-19: New wine needs to be put into new wineskins because old wineskins will break under the pressure new wine creates as it matures. An often overlooked principle we see in this text is that the Lord wants both the new wine and the old wineskins preserved. Old wineskins can still have their place in holding older wine, which is usually more valuable than new wine. Even so, new movements that are represented by

the new wine in this teaching do usually need new containers. At this point in the Lord's ministry, He had not yet raised anyone from the dead, yet here a man comes who has faith for this. This is certainly a "new wine" type of believer.

9:20-22: The high priest's garments had bells and pomegranates attached to the hem of his garment. Pomegranates were used to make medicine and represented healing. The bells spoke of proclamation. When the high priest moved, the pomegranates would strike the bells so the sound would constantly reveal where the high priest was moving. This was prophetic of how whenever Jesus moved, who is the true High Priest, the message of healing would go forth. For the woman to know that all she needed to do was touch the hem of Jesus' garment to be healed was because she obviously recognized that He was the true High Priest of God.

Raising the Nobleman's Daughter

9:23-26: People still scorn when news goes forth of a resurrection, but this is a major sign that accompanies the gospel as a testimony that *the* resurrection is sure, and that there is nothing beyond the power of God to remedy, including death.

Healing the Deaf and Blind

9:27-34: Jesus said to the blind men that it would be done to them according to their faith because He had come to show mankind what our returning to faith in God could accomplish. Faith in ourselves apart from God is the root of all of our problems, and returning to faith in Him is the answer to them.

After Jesus healed the blind men, He healed one who could not speak because he had been bound by a demon. As the people were astonished by this mercy from God, the Pharisees became indignant. We tend to think that if the religious and self-righteous would just see a miracle they would repent, but for those who live in such darkness as legalism and self-righteousness, this is unlikely.

Compassion for the Sheep

9:35-38: When Jesus was moved by compassion for the people who were like sheep without a shepherd, He became their Shepherd. When He was moved by compassion for the people who lived in darkness, He became their teacher. True spiritual authority is founded on compassion.

NOTES

THE GOSPEL OF
MATTHEW
Matthew 10

Apostles First Sent Out

1 When He had called to Himself His twelve disciples, He gave them power over unclean spirits to cast them out, and to heal all kinds of sickness and disease.

2 Now the names of the twelve apostles are: The first, Simon, who is called Peter, and Andrew his brother; James the son of Zebedee, and John his brother;

3 Philip, and Bartholomew; Thomas, and Matthew the tax collector; James the son of Alphaeus, and Lebbaeus, whose surname was Thaddaeus;

4 Simon the Canaanite, and Judas Iscariot, who betrayed Him.

5 These twelve Jesus sent forth and commanded them, saying, "Do not go to the Gentiles or into any city of the Samaritans,

6 "but go to the lost sheep of the house of Israel.

7 "As you go, preach, saying, 'The kingdom of heaven is at hand.'

8 "Heal the sick, cleanse the lepers, raise the dead, cast out devils. Freely you have received, freely give.

9 "Provide neither gold, nor silver, nor brass for your purses,

10 "nor scrip for your journey, neither two coats, or extra shoes, or staves, because the workman is worthy of his wages.

11 "Into whatever city or town you enter, inquire who in it is worthy, and stay with them until you leave.

12 "When you come into a house, give it your greeting of peace.

13 "If the house is worthy, let your peace rest upon it. However, if it is not worthy, let your peace return to you.

14 "Whoever will not receive you, nor hear your message, when you depart from that house, or city, shake off the dust from your feet.

15 "Truly I say to you, it will be more tolerable for the land of Sodom and Gomorrah in the day of judgment than for that city.

16 "I send you forth as sheep into the midst of wolves. Therefore, be wise as serpents, but as harmless as doves.

17 "Beware of men, for they will deliver you up to the courts, and they will scourge you in their synagogues.

18 "You will be brought before governors and kings for My sake as a testimony against them and even before the Gentiles.

19 "When they deliver you up, take no thought for how you will answer or what you will say, because it will be given you at the right time what you are to say.

20 "For it will not be you speaking, but the Spirit of your Father Who will speak through you.

21 "Brother will turn against brother, even to death, and a father against his child. Children will rise up against their parents and cause them to be put to death.

22 "You will be hated by all men for My name's sake, but he that endures to the end will be saved.

23 "When they persecute you in one city, flee to another. Truly I say to you that you will not have gone through the cities of Israel before the Son of Man comes.

24 "The disciple is not above his master, nor the servant above his lord.

25 "It is enough for the disciple that he be as his master, and the servant as his lord. If they have called the master of the house Beelzebub, how much worse shall they call them of his household?

26 "Therefore do not fear them, because there is nothing covered that will not be revealed or hidden that will not be known.

27 "What I tell you in secret speak it in the light. What you hear in your ear, preach upon the housetops.

28 "Do not fear those who can kill the body, but are not able to kill

the soul. Rather fear Him who is able to destroy both soul and body in Gehenna.

29 "Are not two sparrows sold for a penny? Even so, not one of them can fall to the ground without your Father's knowledge.

30 "The very hairs on your head are all numbered.

31 "Therefore fear not. You are more valuable than many sparrows.

Our Cross

32 "Whoever therefore will confess Me before men, I will confess before My Father Who is in heaven.

33 "But whoever will deny Me before men, I will deny him before My Father Who is in heaven.

34 "Do not think that I have come to bring peace on the earth. I did not come to bring peace, but rather a sword.

35 "For I have come to set a man against his father, and the daughter against her mother, and the daughter-in-law against her mother-in-law.

36 "A man's foes will be those of his own household.

37 "He that loves father or mother more than Me is not worthy of Me. He that loves son or daughter more than Me is not worthy of Me.

38 "He that does not take up his cross and follow after Me is not worthy of Me.

39 "He that finds his life will lose it, but he that loses his life for My sake will find it.

Recognizing His Messengers

40 "He that receives you receives Me, and he that receives Me receives Him Who sent Me.

41 "He that receives a prophet in the name of a prophet will receive a prophet's reward. He that receives a righteous man in the name of a righteous man will receive a righteous man's reward.

42 "Whosoever will give a drink of cold water to one of these little ones in the name of a disciple, truly I say to you, he will not lose his reward."

Apostles First Sent Out

Matthew 10:1-31: This is still the way that the Lord sends out His disciples to minister. He not only gave them a responsibility, but He gave them the authority to carry it out. Their basic mission was to help people by setting the oppressed free, healing the sick, and sharing with them the good news of the kingdom of God.

They were not to take provisions for themselves, but rather trust the Lord for His provision since they were sent to do His work. They were to be led by peace, and where they did not find it they were to leave. However, this peace was not an external one, but an internal one as they were to expect persecution. This is because the kingdoms of this world will not easily surrender to the coming kingdom. Even if our families turn against us, we cannot compromise the gospel, keeping in mind that though men may reject us, the Father highly values us. Even though we are promised a great reward for obedience, the Father deserves it, and His gospel deserves it.

Our Cross

10:32-39: This is one of the most clear descriptions of the cost of discipleship. As Bonhoeffer declared, "When the Lord calls a man; He bids Him to come and die." His messengers do live lives of self-sacrifice for the sake of the message, and often they give everything, including their lives. Even so, what they gain is infinitely more.

As we see in John 17 and other places, the Lord's heart for the unity of His people is great. Even so, the gospel will bring a division between His disciples and those who do not follow Him, even to the dividing of families at times. Those who would worship God must love Him above any other relationship, and very often it is at the cost of other relationships. He warned those who would follow Him right up front that this would happen, and we do a great disservice when we do not warn new believers of what they can expect if they remain true to the Lord.

Recognizing His Messengers

10:40-42: It is crucial that we go out in the right way when we are sent. It is crucial that we are able to recognize those who are sent if we are to receive the reward or benefit of their ministry. To do this, we must receive them as if we were receiving the Lord Himself. This was standard as the manner in which an ambassador was received and treated was according to the esteem for the one the ambassador represented.

NOTES

THE GOSPEL OF
MATTHEW
Matthew 11

John the Baptist Questions Jesus

1 When Jesus had finished commanding His twelve disciples, He left to teach and to preach in their cities.

2 Now when John was in prison, he heard of the works of Christ, so he sent two of his disciples and said to Him,

3 "Are You the One that is to come? Or should we look for another?"

4 Jesus answered and said to them, "Go and report to John the things that you have heard and seen:

5 "**'The blind receive their sight, the lame walk, the lepers are cleansed, the deaf hear, the dead are raised up, and the poor have the gospel preached to them'** (Isaiah 35:5-6).

6 "Blessed are those who are not offended by Me."

Jesus Testifies of John

7 As they departed, Jesus said to the multitudes concerning John, "What did you go out into the wilderness to see, a reed shaken by the wind?

8 "What did you go out to see? A man clothed in soft clothing? They that wear soft clothing are in kings' palaces.

9 "What did you go out to see, a prophet? Yes, and I say to you that he was more than a prophet.

10 "For this is he of whom it was written, **'Behold, I send My messenger before your face who shall prepare Your way before you'** (Malachi 3:1).

11 "Truly I say to you among all who have been born of women there has not risen one greater than John the Baptist. Even so, he that is least in the kingdom of heaven is greater than he.

12 "From the days of John the Baptist until now the kingdom of heaven suffers violence, and the violent take it by force,

13 "because all of the prophets and the law prophesied until John.

14 "If you can receive it, this is Elijah who was to come.

15 "He who has ears to hear, let him hear.

16 "But to what will you compare this generation? It is like children sitting in the markets and calling to their friends,

17 "saying, 'We played the flute for you, and you did not dance. We sang a dirge for you, and you did not mourn.'

18 "For John came neither eating nor drinking, and they say, 'He has a demon.'

19 "The Son of Man came eating and drinking, and they say, 'Behold a gluttonous man, and a wine-bibber, a friend of tax collectors and sinners.' Yet wisdom is justified by her children."

Rebuking the Cities of Judea

20 Then He began to chastise the cities in which most of His miracles were done, because they had not repented, saying:

21 "Woe to you, Chorazin! Woe to you, Bethsaida! If the mighty works that were done in you had been done in Tyre and Sidon, they would have repented long ago in sackcloth and ashes.

22 "I say to you, it shall be more tolerable for Tyre and Sidon on the Day of Judgment than for you.

23 "And you, Capernaum, that are exalted to heaven, will be brought down to Hades, because if the mighty works which have been done in you had been done in Sodom it would have remained until this day.

24 "I say to you, it shall be more tolerable for Sodom in the Day of Judgment, than for you."

Rejoicing at Who Will Discern Truth

25 Then Jesus raised His voice, saying, "I thank You and rejoice exceedingly, O Father, Lord of heaven and earth, because You have hidden these things from the wise and intelligent and have revealed them to the very young.

26 "Yes Father, for it seemed good in Your sight.

27 "All things are delivered to Me from My Father, and no man knows the Son, but the Father. Neither does any man know the Father, except the Son, and he to whom the Son chooses to reveal him.

Taking His Yoke

28 "Come to Me all of you that labor and are under heavy burdens, and I will give you rest.

29 "Take My yoke upon you and learn from Me, for I am gentle and humble of heart, and you shall find rest for your souls.

30 "For My yoke is easy, and My burden is light."

John the Baptist Questions Jesus

Matthew 11:1-6, John the Baptist had baptized and testified that Jesus was the Messiah for whom he was preparing the way. Apparently, he began to have doubts when he saw the way Jesus' ministry unfolded, which was very different from John's. This is a trial that every generation likely will go through when the generation emerges that is different. This is also evidence how anyone can, and likely will, battle doubts. Jesus responded to this inquiry patiently, describing how He healed and set people free. Many foresaw the Messiah coming as a great political or military leader, but the true Messiah came loving and helping people.

Jesus Testifies of John

11:7-19: Here Jesus explains that John the Baptist was the prophet who was himself prophesied to come. He would prepare the way for the Messiah and would do this in the spirit

of Elijah. The first prophet, Elijah, had come to turn the hearts of Israel from idols and false gods back to the Lord. This is what John the Baptist came to do in order to prepare them to receive their Messiah. Contrary to Elijah, John did no miracles, but fulfilled his purpose with the power of his message.

John was the last of the old order but the greatest. The new order of the New Covenant, the better covenant, is so superior to the old that the least in the New Covenant would be higher than the greatest of the old.

Then Jesus described how those of the new order would not respond to the music and commands of the old. There is a new liberty and a new sound with the new order. John came living a severe life of fasting, but Jesus came enjoying good food and good wine. Both are misunderstood, but both have their place. Wisdom is for those who feel called to a severe discipline, not to condemn those who appreciate and use the liberty we have in Christ, but not have to emulate it either.

Likewise, those who use their liberty freely must not condemn those who feel called to a different discipline. Those who do not have this grace toward those who live differently can drift toward either legalism or lawlessness. Even so, the New Covenant was not given to be another law and can become an affront to the cross by trying to establish righteousness with works. Those who have the liberty to enjoy good things in moderation, staying within the boundaries of biblical morality, must not condemn those who have chosen a more severe lifestyle. Both have their place, and the most mature can accept and appreciate either. In fact, having both of these in the same body can help promote true spiritual maturity.

A doctrine is promulgated by some that states Jesus did not drink wine, but rather grape juice. This is obviously not the case because why would Jesus be accused of being a drunkard if He were drinking grape juice? The Greek word translated "wine" in the New Testament literally means "fermented grapes," so there is no doubt that it was alcohol. We can contend that Jesus would never have become drunk, or impaired, as He would have certainly lived by the principle of moderation that we are commanded to live in the New Testament, but there is no doubt that He drank wine, not grape juice. For those who have been affected by the tragedy of alcoholism, it is easy to understand why they would have a hard time believing that Jesus would drink wine, but legalism is never the answer to lawlessness. Moderation is often a more powerful witness than abstinence. Twisting the Scriptures, the very Word of God, because of our own prejudices is far more dangerous than alcohol.

Rebuking the Cities of Judea

11:20-24: The cities of Israel that the Lord chastises here were some of the most righteous in the world and possibly of all time. If a person was even caught in adultery they would be stoned, and yet here Jesus said that some of the most perverted and evil cities in history would have it better in the judgment than these cities of Israel. How could this be? Obviously, the severity of the judgment is not based on the depth of evil as much as it is on the degree of light that is rejected. These would have it even more severe in the judgment because they had rejected the greater light. How much light have we been given that we are not living by?

Rejoicing at Who Will Discern Truth

11:25-27: Obviously, human wisdom and intelligence can be a great stumbling block to receiving the truth because of the pride that usually accompanies them. As we are told often, the Lord "resists the proud and gives His grace to the humble." This is something Jesus especially rejoiced in. In the Greek, the exuberance of His rejoicing at this is extraordinary, even indicating that He leapt into the air and spun around because He was so happy about it.

Taking His Yoke

11:28-30: We do not put on a yoke to go to bed, but rather to work. Here we see that when we are engaged in the Lord's work with Him, we will not get tired, but rather refreshed. Nothing in this life is as exhilarating and refreshing as being joined to the Lord in His work.

NOTES

THE GOSPEL OF
MATTHEW
Matthew 12

The Lord of the Sabbath

1 Then Jesus was walking through the grain field on the Sabbath day, and His disciples were hungry, so they began to pluck the grain and to eat it.

2 When the Pharisees saw it, they said to Him, "Your disciples do that which is not lawful to do on the Sabbath day.

3 So He said to them, "Have you not read what David did, when he was hungry, and they that were with him?

4 "He entered into the house of God and ate the show-bread which was not lawful for him to eat, or for those who were with him, but only for the priests?

5 "Or have you not read in the law, how that on the Sabbath days the priests in the temple work on the Sabbath and are blameless?

6 "I say to you, there is One in this place greater than the temple.

7 "If you had known what this means, 'I desire mercy rather than sacrifice,' you would not have condemned the innocent.

8 "For the Son of Man is Lord of the Sabbath."

Healing on the Sabbath

9 He then departed and went into their synagogue.

10 There was a man whose hand had withered so they asked Him, "Is it lawful to heal on the Sabbath?" They asked Him this so that they could accuse Him.

11 He said to them, "Who is there among you that has a sheep, and if it fell into a pit on the Sabbath day, would not rescue it?

12 "How much more important is a man than a sheep? Therefore it is lawful to do good on the Sabbath."

13 Then He said to the man, "Stretch out your hand." So he stretched it out and it was restored completely just like the other.

14 Then the Pharisees went out, and held a council to determine how they might destroy Him.

15 When Jesus found out about it, He withdrew from there, and great multitudes followed Him, and He healed them all,

16 and charged them not to make Him known,

17 so that it might be fulfilled which was spoken through Isaiah the prophet, saying,

18 **"Behold My servant, whom I have chosen; My beloved Son in Him I am well pleased. I will put my Spirit upon Him, and He will declare justice to the Gentiles.**

19 **"He will not strive, nor cry out, and neither will His voice be heard in the streets.**

20 **"A bruised reed He will not break, and smoking flax He shall not quench, until He leads justice to victory.**

21 **"In His name the Gentiles will trust"** (Isaiah 42:1-4).

A House Divided

22 Then one possessed with a devil was brought to Him who was blind and dumb, and He healed him so that the blind and dumb both spoke and saw.

23 All the people were amazed and said, "Is this not the Son of David?"

24 When the Pharisees heard it, they said, "This fellow casts out demons by Beelzebub the prince of the demons."

25 Jesus, knowing their thoughts, said to them, "Every kingdom divided against itself will be brought down and come to nothing. Neither can any city or house divided against itself stand.

26 "If Satan casts out Satan, he is divided against himself. How then will his kingdom stand?

27 "If I cast out devils by Beelzebub, by whom do your children cast them out? Therefore they will be your judges.

28 "If I cast out devils by the Spirit of God, then the kingdom of God has come upon you.

29 "Or how can one enter into a strong man's house and steal his goods unless he first binds the strong man, and then he can rob his house.

We Are Either for or Against Him

30 "He that is not with Me is against Me, and he that does not gather with Me scatters abroad.

31 "Therefore I say to you that all manner of sin and blasphemy will be forgiven men, but blasphemy against the Holy Spirit will not be forgiven men.

32 "So, whoever speaks a word against the Son of Man it will be forgiven him, but whoever speaks against the Holy Spirit it will not be forgiven him, neither in this age, nor in the age to come.

33 "Either make the tree good and its fruit good, or else make the tree corrupt and its fruit corrupt, because a tree is known by his fruit.

34 "O generation of vipers, how can you, being evil, speak good things? For out of the abundance of what is in the heart the mouth speaks.

35 "A good man out of the good treasure of the heart brings forth good things, and an evil man out of the evil treasure brings forth evil things.

36 "I say to you that every idle word that men shall speak they shall give account of in the Day of Judgment.

37 "For by your words you will be justified, and by your words you will be condemned."

Seeking a Sign

38 Then some of the scribes and the Pharisees spoke up and said, "Master, we want to see You perform a miracle."

39 So He answered them, saying, "An evil and adulterous generation seeks after a miracle, and no miracle will be given to it except the sign of the prophet Jonah.

40 "For just as Jonah was in the whale's belly for three days and three nights, so will the Son of Man be three days and three nights in the heart of the earth.

41 "The men of Nineveh will arise in judgment against this generation and will condemn it because they repented at the preaching of Jonah, and One greater than Jonah is here.

42 "The queen of the south will rise up in the judgment with this generation and will condemn it because she came from the uttermost parts of the earth to hear the wisdom of Solomon, and One greater than Solomon is here.

The Strategy of Unclean Spirits

43 "When the unclean spirit has gone out of a man, he wanders through dry places seeking rest and finds none.

44 "Then it says, 'I will return into my house from which I came out.' When it comes back, it finds it empty, swept, and put in order.

45 So it then goes and gets seven other spirits more wicked than itself, and they enter in and dwell there. Then the last state of that man is worse than the first. Even so shall it be with this wicked generation."

His True Family

46 While He was talking to the people, His mother and His brothers stood close by, wanting to speak with Him.

47 Then one said to Him, "Behold, Your mother and Your brothers are wanting to speak with You."

48 He said to the one who told Him this, "Who is My mother? Who are My brethren?"

49 He then stretched forth His hand toward His disciples, and said, "Behold My mother and My brethren!

50 "For whoever will do the will of My Father who is in heaven, he is My brother, and sister, and mother."

The Lord of the Sabbath

Matthew 12:1-8: The law was made for man, not the other way around. The Lord is not as harsh and controlling as some legalistic people are who think they are representing Him.

The Sabbath day that the Lord is referring to here is not just the last day of the week, but His one thousand-year reign on earth. As Peter and some of the other early church fathers wrote, "with the Lord a day is as a thousand years." Therefore, a thousand years is often referred to as a "prophetic day." If you calculate from the genealogies in Scripture, it has now been about six thousand years since Adam, or six prophetic days. We are therefore close to the time when Christ will come to rule over the earth for a thousand years, which will also be the prophetic Sabbath.

Healing on the Sabbath

12:9-21: Legalism does terrible things to the hearts of people, such as trying to forbid the Lord from healing on the Sabbath while they would all rescue one of their animals if needed on the Sabbath.

Here we see again that even if the legalists see a great miracle, it will not likely penetrate their hard hearts. As He still does today, He often departs from such leaders to move among the common people.

A House Divided

12:22-29: The more power that Jesus demonstrated, the more outrageous the accusations of the legalists became. Yet Jesus patiently taught them wisdom from above even if they would not receive it. An ultimate wisdom is that division destroys and unity can bring victory. Is it not time for His people to hear this?

He also explained that if we want the kingdom to come to a situation, we must cast the darkness out with the Spirit of God. Satan will not cast out Satan, so we must respond in the fruit of the Spirit, not the same spirit that is attacking us.

We Are Either for or Against Him

12:30-37: To determine what spirit one is moving in, we must look at their fruit because many deceivers claim to be Christians. Does their ministry draw people to Christ and Christlikeness, or do they cause division, strife, or impart fear instead of faith?

There are serious consequences for our words because words can have the power of death and life in them (see Proverbs 18:21). With them we can either impart life and faith to people, or fear, doubts, and death. We must think of our tongues as a weapon for good or evil, and we will be held accountable for how we use it.

Seeking a Sign

12:38-42: Again, referring to the standard of judgment being based more on the amount of light that is rejected than the degree of inequity, our cities and nations today may think that they are doing well because of the degree of their civility and civilization. However, the standard set in Scripture in history is how some of these most wicked of all nations, such as Nineveh, then repented at the preaching of a wayward prophet with a bad attitude. Some of the greatest pastors, teachers, preachers, and missionaries live in our times. How have the nations today responded to them?

The Strategy of Unclean Spirits

12:43-45: A demon that is cast out will always seek to return, and those who experience deliverance must be prepared for this or they can end up in a worse condition. Whatever we get free from that has had a grip on us, we must resolve not to open the door to it again.

This same principle is also true with principalities and powers over regions. When we have campaigns and crusades to confront and cast out darkness in a region, we must resolve to also hold this territory against a sure counterattack by the evil seeking to return. We must fill the void immediately with the nature of the Holy Spirit that is the counter to the evil displaced.

His True Family

12:46-50: Contrary to the way this may seem at first, this was not a dishonoring of His mother, who Jesus always showed the greatest honor, esteem, and affection for. However, here He is broadening the perspective of those who bore Him and who are His true family members as being the obedient seekers of God. The obedient true seekers of God in Israel had all been a part of carrying the seed of Christ and being His true family. The obedient true seekers of God in every generation still have this privilege.

NOTES

THE GOSPEL OF
MATTHEW
Matthew 13

Parable of the Sower

1 The same day Jesus went out of the house and sat down at the seashore,

2 and great multitudes gathered about Him, so He got into a ship and sat while the multitude stood on the shore.

3 Then He spoke to them many things in parables, saying, "Behold, a sower went out to sow seed.

4 "As he sowed, some seed fell by the side of the road, and the birds came and devoured them.

5 "Some of the seed fell upon rocky soil and sprung up quickly because they had no depth.

6 "But when the sun came up, they were scorched, and because they had no root they withered quickly.

7 "Some fell among thorns, and the thorns sprung up, and choked them.

8 "But some fell onto good ground and brought forth fruit, some a hundredfold, some sixty-fold, and some thirty-fold.

9 "Let the one who has ears to hear, let him hear."

Understanding the Mysteries

10 Then the disciples came and said to Him, "Why do You speak to them in parables?"

11 He answered and said to them, "Because it has been given to you

to understand the mysteries of the kingdom of heaven, but to them it has not been given.

12 "For whoever has, to him shall more be given, and he will have an even greater abundance. Whoever does not have, it shall be taken from him even what he has.

13 "Therefore I speak to them in parables, because seeing they do not see, and hearing they do not hear, neither do they understand."

14 "In them is the prophecy of Isaiah is fulfilled that says, **'Even though you hear you will not understand, and even though you see you do not perceive:**

15 **'For the heart's of this people have become hard, and their ears are dull of hearing, and their eyes they have closed; lest at any time they should see with their eyes, and hear with their ears, and should understand with their heart, and should be converted, and I should heal them'"** (Isaiah 6:9-10).

16 "Blessed are your eyes because they see and your ears because they hear.

17 "For truly I say to you that many prophets and righteous men have desired to see the things that you see, and have not seen them, and to hear those things that you hear, and have not heard them.

18 "Therefore listen to the meaning of this parable of the sower.

19 "When any one hears the word of the kingdom, and does not understand it, then the wicked one comes, and steals away that which was sown in his heart. This is the one that received seed by the road side.

20 "The one who received the seed on stony soil is the one that hears the word and receives it with joy,

21 "yet does not have enough depth in himself for the word to take root, so he only endures until tribulation or persecution arises because of the word, and then they become offended.

22 "The one that receives the seed among the thorns is one that hears the word, and the cares of this world, and the deceitfulness of riches, choke the word, and they become unfruitful.

23 "The one that receives the seed into the good ground is one that hears the word and understands it so that it takes deep root, and

therefore bears fruit, bringing forth, some a hundredfold, some sixty, and some thirty."

Parable of the Wheat and Tares

24 Then He spoke another parable to them, saying, "The kingdom of heaven is like a man that sowed good seed in his field,

25 "but at night his enemy came and sowed tares among the wheat and slipped away.

26 "When the seed sprouted and brought forth fruit, then tares appeared also.

27 "So the servants of the landowner came and said to him, 'Sir, did you not sow good seed in your field? Where did these tares come from?'

28 "He said to them, 'An enemy has done this.' The servants then said to him, 'Will you then go and gather them up?'

29 "He said, 'No. If you gather up the tares, you will also root up the wheat with them.

30 'Let both grow together until the harvest. At the time of harvest I will say to the reapers, 'Gather up the tares first, and bind them in bundles to burn them, and then gather the wheat into my barn.'"

Parable of the Mustard Seed

31 Then He shared with them another parable, saying, "The kingdom of heaven is like a grain of mustard seed that a man took and sowed in his field:

32 "It is the smallest of all seeds, but when it is grown it is the greatest among herbs, becoming a tree so that the birds come and lodge in the branches of it."

Parable of the Leaven

33 Then He spoke another parable to them; "The kingdom of heaven is like leaven that a woman took and hid in three measures of meal until the whole of it was leavened."

34 All these things Jesus spoke to the multitude in parables, and except through parables He did not speak to them,

35 so that it might be fulfilled that was spoken by the prophet, saying, **"I will open My mouth in parables; I will utter things that have been kept secret from the foundation of the world"** (Psalm 78:2).

Explaining the Wheat and Tares

36 Then Jesus sent the multitude away, and went into the house, and His disciples came to Him, saying, "Explain to us the parable of the tares of the field."

37 He answered them, "He that sows the good seed is the Son of Man.

38 "The field is the world. The good seed are the children of the kingdom, but the tares are the children of the wicked one.

39 "The enemy that sowed them is the devil. The harvest is the end of the age, and the reapers are the messengers.

40 "As the tares are gathered and burned in the fire, that is how it will be at the end of this age.

41 "The Son of Man will send forth his messengers, and they will gather out of His kingdom all things that offend, and those who practice lawlessness,

42 "and will cast them into a furnace of fire. There will be wailing and gnashing of teeth.

43 "Then the righteous will shine forth as the sun in the kingdom of their Father. Let the one who has ears to hear, hear.

The Kingdom Is the Treasure

44 "Again, the kingdom of heaven is like a treasure hidden that a man finds in a field, who then with great joy goes and sells all that he has and buys that field.

45 "Again, the kingdom of heaven is like a merchant who is seeking the best pearls,

46 "and when he found one pearl of great value, he went and sold all that he had to buy it.

The Dragnet

47 "The kingdom of heaven is like a net that was cast into the sea and gathered every kind of *sea creature.*

48 "When the net was full, they drew it to shore, and they sat down and gathered the good into vessels, but cast the bad away.

49 "This is what it will be like at the end of the age. The messengers will come forth and separate the wicked from among the just,

50 "and will cast them into the furnace of fire. There will be wailing and gnashing of teeth."

51 Jesus said to them, "Have you understood all of these things?" They replied, "Yes, Lord."

The Wise Scribe

52 Then He said to them, "Therefore every scribe that is instructed in the ways of the kingdom of heaven is like a man that is a householder who brings forth from his treasure things new and old."

53 So it came about that when Jesus had finished these parables, He departed.

His Neighbors Offended

54 When He had come into His own country, He taught them in their synagogue. They were astonished and said, "Where did this man get this wisdom and these mighty works?

55 "Is this not the carpenter's son? Is not His mother called Mary? Are not His brethren, James, and Joseph, and Simon, and Judas?

56 "His sisters, are they not all with us? Where did this man get all of these things?"

57 So they were offended at Him. Therefore Jesus said to them, "A prophet is not without honor except in his own country, and in his own house."

58 So He did not do many miracles there because of their unbelief.

Parable of the Sower

Matthew 13:1-9: The Parable of the Sower is a profound but simple truth about those who will bear fruit for the kingdom. What kind of soil are we? If we are not the good soil that bears fruit with what is sown, how can we change so that we can bear fruit? This parable tells us how.

The seed that was sown beside the road was where people often traveled. Do people easily trample what is sown in our hearts so that it is easily plucked up?

The rocky soil is hard, resistant to the Word. Are we so critical that it is hard for the Word of God to penetrate our hearts?

The thorns are explained to be the cares and worries of this world. What in this life has taken a higher priority with us than knowing God's truth and doing God's will?

The good soil gladly receives the Word as the treasure that it is, being well-prepared to nurture and water it so that it will grow and bear fruit. Prepared soil takes effort. It must be broken up and kept loose to receive the seed. The stones and other plants that would sap the nutrients must be constantly weeded out. Only those who really keep Him as their first love will make this effort. Those are the ones who are bearing fruit.

Understanding the Mysteries

13:10-23: Here we see that the Lord did not make it easy for people to understand His teaching, but purposely made it hard. He does this to separate those who will receive His Words from those who will not because of the issues He taught in the Parable of the Sower. Only those who care enough to become "good soil" and treasure His Word are worthy of understanding.

Parable of the Wheat and Tares

13:24-30: See verses 36-43 below.

Parable of the Mustard Seed

13:31-32: Faith is a seed. This means that anything done in

faith can grow into something far greater. Like any seed, to grow it needs to be sown into good soil, watered, which is the Word of God, it needs sunlight, which is the right spiritual climate, and it needs to have the other encroaching plants that could choke it out kept away, which are the cares and worries of this world. The first job given to man was to cultivate. Cultivating that which is sown by the Word of God into our hearts is the most important cultivation of all. If we want great faith, then we must give it the attention it deserves.

Parable of the Leaven

13:33-35: That the kingdom is like leaven means that just a tiny bit of it sown into the right circumstances can spread far. How is the revelation of the kingdom spreading that we have been given?

Explaining the Wheat and Tares

13:36-43: Tares look like wheat, but they are noxious. Here we see that wheat and tares are sown in the same field. Many church leaders spend much effort trying to separate the wheat and tares in their church, but they are hard to distinguish until they have both matured. Those who try to separate them prematurely often get rid of the wheat and keep the tares. God's wisdom is to let them grow up together. The sowing of these tares among the wheat obviously could not happen without the Lord allowing it, so we need to understand how dealing with the tares growing in the midst of the wheat is part of His curriculum. This is why He placed Judas in the midst of His own disciples even though He knew who Judas was. In the fullness of time, the nature of Judas was revealed.

At the harvest, the time of maturity, wheat bows over, or becomes more humble. Tares will stand straight. Pride and humility are the distinguishing characteristics of the tares and the wheat, but this will only be fully revealed when both are mature.

We also see here that at the harvest the tares will be gathered into bundles first. Jesus later explains that the harvest is the end of the age. The end of this age will be the greatest ingathering of souls into the kingdom, but it also will be the time when the tares gather together as well. The harvest is the reaping of everything that has been sown in man, both the good and the evil, the light and the darkness. These, and the conflict between them, will increase as we get closer to the end of the age.

The Kingdom is the Treasure

13:44-46: The kingdom is worth giving up everything else that we have to pursue.

The Dragnet

13:47-51: There are evangelists today who are gathering great harvests all over the earth. Even though multitudes may make decisions for Christ in these crusades, it seems that only a small fraction of them are added to the church and bear fruit for the kingdom. This is what was prophesied here—the evangelists are throwing dragnets. Even so, if these works were followed up by apostles and prophets, as demonstrated in the Book of Acts, we would likely have far more added to the church and bearing fruit for the kingdom.

The Wise Scribe

13:52-53: Many gravitate toward the new things that God is doing and seem in endless pursuit of something new. Others gravitate to the more traditional and established. The wise do both, sinking their roots deeper and deeper into sound biblical truth, while also being open to new revelation and insight from the Lord.

His Neighbors Offended

13:54-58: "Familiarity breeds contempt" is a common saying and is often true. Judas was familiar with Jesus, but John was an intimate friend. Which are we?

It is an amazing thing that doubt could keep Jesus from doing His works. It does because the Holy Spirit is the Helper, not the Doer. When the Lord delegated authority over the earth to man, He will only move on the earth through those who want Him. So for God to do His work on the earth, He needs someone to join with Him in faith.

NOTES

THE GOSPEL OF
MATTHEW
Matthew 14

John the Baptist Martyred

1 At that time Herod the tetrarch heard of the fame of Jesus,

2 and said to his servants, "This is John the Baptist. He has risen from the dead, and that is why these miraculous powers work through him."

3 This is because Herod had arrested John, bound him, and put him in prison for Herodias' sake, who had been his brother Philip's wife.

4 John had said to him, "It is not lawful for you to have her."

5 So he wanted to have him put to death, but he feared the multitude, because they considered him to be a prophet.

6 When Herod's birthday was celebrated, the daughter of Herodias danced before them and pleased Herod.

7 So he promised her with an oath to give her whatever she asked for.

8 So being instructed by her mother, she said, "Give me the head of John the Baptist in a charger."

9 The king was grieved, but for the sake of the oath he had given before those who were attending the dinner, he commanded that it to be given to her.

10 So he had John beheaded in the prison.

11 Then his head was brought in a charger and given to the young girl, and she brought it to her mother.

12 His disciples came and took his body and buried it and went and told Jesus.

13 When Jesus heard of it, He departed there by ship into a desert place to be alone. However, when the people had heard where He was, they followed Him on foot from their cities.

Feeding the Five Thousand

14 When Jesus saw the great multitude, He was moved with compassion for them, and so He healed their sick.

15 When it was evening, His disciples came to Him, saying, "This is a desert place, and it is late. Send the multitude away so that they can go into the villages and buy food for themselves."

16 Jesus then said to them, "They do not need to depart. You give them food to eat."

17 So the disciples said to Him, "We only have five loaves, and two fish here."

18 He said, "Bring them here to Me."

19 After He commanded the multitude to sit down on the grass, He took the five loaves and the two fish, and looking up to heaven, He blessed them, broke them, and handed the loaves to His disciples, and the disciples started giving them to the multitude.

20 So they all ate until they were filled. Then they took up the fragments that were left over and there were twelve baskets full.

21 The number of those who had eaten were about five thousand men, besides the women and children.

Walking on Water

22 Immediately Jesus told His disciples to get into a boat and to go before Him to the other side, while He sent the multitudes away.

23 When He had sent the multitudes away, He went up into a mountain alone to pray. When evening had come, He was there alone.

24 Yet the boat was now in the middle of the sea and was being tossed by the waves because the wind was contrary.

25 In the fourth watch of the night [between 3:00 a.m. and 6:00 a.m.], Jesus approached them walking on the sea.

26 When the disciples saw Him walking on the sea, they were terrified and cried out in fear, saying, "It is a spirit!"

27 Quickly Jesus spoke to them, saying, "Do not be afraid. Have courage. It is Me."

28 Peter then said to Him, "Lord, if it is You, call me to come to You on the water."

29 He said, "Come." So Peter got out of the boat, and he walked on the water to go to Jesus.

30 However, when he saw the wind blowing he became frightened, and began to sink, so he cried, saying, "Lord, save me!"

31 Jesus reached out and caught him, and said to him, "O you of little faith! Why did you doubt?"

32 When they got into the boat, the wind ceased.

33 Then those who were in the boat came and worshiped Him, saying, "It is certainly true that You are the Son of God."

34 When they had crossed over they were in the land of Gennesaret.

35 The men of that place heard that He was there; they sent out into all of the surrounding country, and brought to Him all that were diseased.

36 Then they asked Him to just let them touch the hem of His garment, and as many as touched it were made perfectly well.

John the Baptist Martyred

Matthew 14:1-14: We may wonder why the Lord would let His prophet be so cruelly imprisoned and killed in this way, yet to have remained faithful to his calling and then to suffer martyrdom is one of the highest honors the servants of the Lord can have. These are the ones who do not count even their own lives in this world as having value compared to the life that they have eternally with the Lord in heaven. This was John's crown for a life well lived by giving it to the Lord and His purposes.

Feeding the Five Thousand

14:14-21: Every miracle of Jesus is a message, and the basic message of every miracle is that the kingdom of heaven has authority over any condition on the earth. As we grow in the Lord so as to abide in the King and He abides in us, we too will have this authority.

Walking on Water

14:22-26: I once had a dream in which the Lord said to me that He was going to show me how to do the "greater works." He said that Peter did not walk on the water, but he walked on His Word. When He said to Peter "Come," that Word had more substance than the firmament. If the Lord says to us to walk on the air, then we can walk on it easier than we could on solid earth.

I was also shown that what we pray for is often not received because we put our faith in an outcome instead of in the Lord. True faith is seeing Jesus, who He is, and where He sits above all rule and dominion and authority. For this reason, Peter was doing fine walking on the water as long as he kept his attention on Jesus. When we see Him and are obeying Him, we can walk above any circumstances. When Peter took his eyes off of Jesus and started looking at the waves, he sank, just as we do when we take our eyes off of Jesus.

Their vessel, the boat, was being tossed about by contrary winds. As soon as Jesus got into the boat, the winds stopped and they were immediately at their destination. When we are faced with contrary circumstances, we do not need to focus on making them go away as much as we need to focus on the Lord and bringing Him into our situation. He does not just have the answer to every human problem—He is the answer to every human problem.

NOTES

THE GOSPEL OF
MATTHEW
Matthew 15

The Source of Defilements

1 Then scribes and Pharisees from Jerusalem came to Jesus, saying,

2 "Why do Your disciples transgress the tradition of the elders? For they do not wash their hands before they eat."

3 He answered and said to them, "Why do you transgress the commandment of God with your traditions?

4 "For God gave the commandment, **'Honor your father and mother,'** and 'He that curses father or mother must die.'

5 "But you say, 'Whoever will say to his father or his mother, 'What I had that could have helped you I have given to another,'

6 "and those who neglect to honor his father or his mother in this way shall be free. In this way you have made the commandment of God to have no effect because of your tradition.

7 "You hypocrites! Isaiah said it well when he prophesied of you:

8 **"'This people draw near to Me with their mouth, and honor Me with their words, but their heart is far from Me.'**

9 **"'It is in vain that they worship Me, teaching for doctrines the commandments of men'"** (Isaiah 29:13).

10 He then called the multitude, and said to them, "Hear, and understand:

11 "It is not that which goes into the mouth that defiles a man, but what comes out of the mouth, this is what defiles a man."

12 Then came His disciples, and said to Him, "Do You not know that the Pharisees were offended after they heard this saying?"

13 He answered, "Every plant that My heavenly Father has not planted will be rooted up.

14 "Do not be concerned about them. They are blind leaders of the blind. If the blind lead the blind, both will fall into the ditch."

15 Then Peter said to Him, "Tell us the meaning of this parable."

16 Jesus replied, saying, "Do you still not have understanding?

17 "Do you not yet understand that whatever enters into the mouth goes into the stomach and is then eliminated?

18 "But those things that proceed out of the mouth come forth from the heart, and they defile the man.

19 "For out of the heart proceeds evil thoughts, murders, adulteries, fornications, thefts, false witness, and blasphemies.

20 "These are the things that defile a man, but to eat with unwashed hands do not defile a man."

The Canaanite Woman

21 Then Jesus departed for the coasts of Tyre and Sidon.

22 A woman from Canaan came out of the same coasts, and cried to Him, saying, "Have mercy on me, O Lord, Son of David. My daughter is grievously oppressed by a devil."

23 He did not respond to her with so much as a word. His disciples then came and said to Him, "Send her away because she will not stop crying after us."

24 So He answered and said, "I have only been sent to the lost sheep of the house of Israel."

25 Then she came and worshiped Him and said, "Lord, help me."

26 He then answered her saying, "It is not right to take the children's food and give it to dogs."

27 She replied, "That is true, Lord, but even the dogs eat the crumbs that fall from their masters' table."

28 Then Jesus answered and said to her, "O woman, your faith is great. It will be done for you just as you have desired." So her daughter was made well at that very moment.

Feeding the Multitude a Second Time

29 Jesus then departed from there, and came near to the Sea of Galilee, and went up into a mountain and sat down there.

30 Then a great multitude came to Him, having brought those that were lame, blind, dumb, maimed, and many others, and laid them down at Jesus' feet; and He healed them.

31 The multitude was in awe as they saw the dumb speak, the maimed made whole, the lame to walk, and the blind begin to see, and so they glorified the God of Israel.

32 Then Jesus called His disciples to Him, and said, "I feel compassion for the multitude because they have been with Me for three days now and have nothing to eat. I do not want to send them away fasting, or they may faint on the way."

33 His disciples said to Him, "Where could we get enough bread in the wilderness to feed so great a multitude?"

34 Jesus said to them, "How many loaves do you have?" They replied, "Seven, and just a few little fishes."

35 So He commanded the multitude to sit down on the ground.

36 He took the seven loaves and the fishes and gave thanks, and broke them and gave them to His disciples to distribute to the multitude.

37 So they all ate until they were filled. Then they took up the leftovers and there were seven baskets full.

38 Those who ate were four thousand men, plus the women and children.

39 Then He sent the multitude away and took a ship to the coasts of Magadan.

The Source of Defilements

Matthew 15:1-20: It is the nature of the evil religious spirit to be more devoted to the law than to the people for whom the law was given. Legalism kills love, and loving God and one another are always the two greatest commandments. An inordinate devotion to the law results in men inventing increasingly strict ways that the law must be kept. Then these

traditions can become more of an occupation than the law itself, and the slide into the dark hole of legalism goes deeper and deeper.

The Canaanite Woman

15:21-28: Here we see faith penetrating through the barrier of the law to touch God's heart and receive help for her daughter. Faith and love can overcome any barrier and will arrest God's heart. This is one of two people who Jesus said had "great faith." The other, the Centurion, was also a Gentile. Could it be that they could touch faith in a higher way because they were not burdened by the law?

Feeding the Multitude a Second Time

15:29-39: Jesus had the greatest gift of hospitality of all-time, and it compelled Him to do miracles to provide food for those who came to see and hear Him. Those who come to Him will have the provisions they need.

NOTES

THE GOSPEL OF
MATTHEW
Matthew 16

Discerning the Times

1 Then the Pharisees and Sadducees came in order to tempt Him, asking if He would show them a sign from heaven,

2 so He said to them: "When it is evening you say, 'It will be fair weather, because the sky is red.'

3 "In the morning you say, 'It will be foul weather today, because the sky is red and threatening.' You hypocrites! Can you discern the face of the sky, but you cannot discern the signs of the times?

4 "A wicked and adulterous generation seeks after a sign. There will be no sign given to it, but the sign of the prophet Jonah." So He withdrew from them, and departed.

The Leaven of Legalism

5 When His disciples came to the other side they had forgotten to take bread.

6 Then Jesus said to them, "Take heed to what I am about to tell you—beware of the leaven of the Pharisees and of the Sadducees."

7 So they reasoned among themselves, saying, "It is because we did not bring bread."

8 When Jesus perceived this, He said to them, "O you of little faith! Why do you reason among yourselves about not bringing the bread?

9 "Do you not yet understand or remember the five loaves of bread that we fed five thousand with? How many baskets were left over?

10 "Or do you not remember how the seven loaves fed the four thousand, and how many baskets did we have left?

11 "How is it that you do not understand that I am not talking to you about bread, but that you should beware of the leaven of the Pharisees and of the Sadducees?"

12 Then they understood that He was not warning them to beware of the leaven of bread, but of the teachings of the Pharisees and of the Sadducees.

The Great Testimony

13 When Jesus came to the coasts of Caesarea Philippi, He asked His disciples, saying, "Who do men say that I, the Son of Man, am?"

14 They said, "Some say that You are John the Baptist, some say Elijah, and others Jeremiah, or one of the prophets."

15 Then He said to them, "But who do you say that I am?"

16 Simon Peter answered and said, "You are the Christ, the Son of the living God."

17 Jesus then said to him, "Blessed are you, Simon, son of Jonah, because flesh and blood did not reveal this to you, but My Father who is in heaven.

18 "I say to you Peter that upon this rock I will build My church, and the gates of hell will not prevail against it.

19 "I will give to you the keys of the kingdom of heaven, and whatever you will bind on earth shall be bound in heaven, and whatever you will loose on earth shall be loosed in heaven."

20 Then He charged His disciples that they should tell no man that He was the Christ.

Preparing for the Cross

21 From that time on Jesus began to show His disciples how He had to go to Jerusalem, and suffer many things from the elders, the chief priests, and scribes, and be killed, and be raised again the third day.

22 Then Peter took Him aside, and began to rebuke Him, saying, "This cannot be allowed. It must not happen to You!"

23 He turned, and said to Peter, "Get behind Me, Satan! You are a

stumbling block to Me because you are not setting your mind on God's interests, but on the interests of men."

24 Then Jesus said to His disciples, "If any man wants to follow Me, let him deny himself, and take up his cross, and follow Me.

25 "Because whoever seeks to save his life will lose it, and whoever is willing to lose his life for My sake will find it.

26 "For what is a man profited if he gains the whole world, but loses his own soul? Or what will a man give in exchange for his soul?

27 "For the Son of Man will come in the glory of His Father, with His angels, and then He will reward every man according to his works.

28 "Truly I say to you, there are those standing here who will not taste of death until they see the Son of Man coming in His kingdom."

Discerning the Times

Matthew 16:1-4: The Lord called them a "wicked and adulterous generation" because they came seeking a sign from heaven. A sign "from heaven" was asking Jesus to do something like Joshua did when he stopped the sun. Jesus could have done this, but His signs were not just to prove that He had power, but to reveal the heart of God. The works of Jesus were motivated by His love for people. He wanted to see them well and free from oppression and provide their needs. The reason why the Lord rebuked them for this question was because it revealed how out of touch they were with the message of His signs. Then He turned the conversation to the signs of the times because this was the major issue that they were missing.

The Leaven of Legalism

16:5-12: Leaven causes fermentation in dough, which is an agitation. This is the nature of legalism when it is in teaching—it causes an agitation, lack of rest, lack of peace, and instead a striving because no one can ever measure up to the standards of legalism.

The Great Testimony

16:13-20: The "rock" that Jesus will build His church on is revelation from the Father of who Jesus is. It can be helpful to get the opinions of other people, but when the Father reveals something to us it cannot be shaken—it is a rock. No one will be saved because they believed someone else's opinion of who Jesus is, but we are told that no one comes to the Son unless the Father draws them. When He draws us to His Son, it may come through other people. However, it is His anointing that penetrates not just to the mind, but also to the heart. In Romans 10:10, we are told that it is with the heart that man must believe if it is to result in righteousness. When we believe in our hearts, it changes our lives, not just our opinions. This is a key to living in the kingdom that is the solid rock that cannot be shaken.

Preparing for the Cross

16:21-28: The life built on the Rock is also a life of sacrifice, taking up the cross and denying ourselves to do His will.

Just after receiving the great commendation in Scripture for having the revelation of who Jesus is, and being given the keys to the kingdom, Peter then hears straight from hell and receives one of the worst rebukes in Scripture. The point is that many who create the great advances will also be prone to some of the biggest mistakes. Even so, the Lord did not take the keys away from Peter after this blunder, but Peter would use them. He would also make more mistakes. If we're too afraid of making mistakes to step out, we will not accomplish much. If we have the faith to step out, we will likely need the faith to get up after we've stumbled and keep going. "The righteous falls seven times but rises yet again" (see Proverbs 24:10). Possibly the greatest faith is to get up and keep going after a mistake.

NOTES

The Gospel of
MATTHEW
Matthew 17

The Mountain of Transfiguration

1 Six days later Jesus took Peter, James, and John his brother, and brought them up into a high mountain alone.

2 There He was transfigured before them, and His face shone like the sun, and His clothing became as white as light.

3 Then Moses and Elijah appeared to them, talking with Him.

4 So Peter answered and said to Jesus, "Lord, it is good for us to be here. If You are willing, let us make three tabernacles here: one for You, one for Moses, and one for Elijah."

5 While he was still speaking a bright cloud overshadowed them, and a voice came out of the cloud, saying, "This is My beloved Son, in whom I am well pleased. Listen to Him."

6 When the disciples heard it, they fell on their faces and were very afraid.

7 Then Jesus came and touched them, saying, "Arise, and do not be afraid."

8 When they looked up they saw no one except Jesus Himself, alone.

Understanding Elijah

9 As they came down from the mountain Jesus charged them, saying, "Tell the vision to no one until the Son of Man has risen from the dead."

10 So His disciples asked Him, saying, "Why do the scribes say that Elijah must come first?"

11 Jesus answered, "It is true that Elijah will come first and restore all things.

12 "But I say to you that Elijah has already come, and they did not recognize him, but did to him whatever they desired. In the same way, the Son of Man will suffer at their hands."

13 Then the disciples understood that He spoke to them of John the Baptist.

Casting out Demons

14 When they had come to the multitude, a certain man came up to Him, knelt, and said,

15 "Lord, have mercy on my son because he is insane and terribly oppressed. He often falls into the fire and into the water.

16 "I brought him to Your disciples, but they could not set him free."

17 Then Jesus answered and said, "O faithless and perverse generation. How long will I be with you? How long must I suffer you? Bring him here to Me."

18 Then Jesus rebuked the devil, and it departed from him, and the child was healed at that very moment.

19 The disciples then came to Jesus in private and said, "Why could we not cast it out?"

20 Jesus said to them, "Because of your unbelief. For it is true that if you have faith as a grain of mustard seed, you would be able to say to this mountain, 'Be lifted up and moved over to that place,' and it would move, and nothing would be impossible to you.

21 "Even so, this kind does not go out except by prayer and fasting."

22 While they stayed in Galilee, Jesus said to them, "The Son of Man will be betrayed into the hands of men.

23 "They will kill Him, and the third day He will rise again." So they were deeply grieved.

Fishing for Taxes

24 When they had come to Capernaum, the officials who received the tribute money came to Peter and said, "Does your Master not pay the tribute?"

25 He said, "Yes." When they had come into the house, before he could speak, Jesus said, "What do you think, Simon? From whom do the kings of the earth take custom or tribute? From their own children, or from strangers?"

26 Peter said to Him, "From strangers." Jesus then said, "Then the children are free from this tax.

27 "However, so that we do not offend them, go to the sea, and cast in a hook, and take up the first fish that comes up. When you have opened its mouth, you will find a piece of money. Take it, and give it to them for you and Me."

The Mountain of Transfiguration

Matthew 17:1-8: Moses represents the law and Elijah the prophets. This transfiguration speaks of how both the law and prophets spoke of Jesus. However, Peter wanted to make a tabernacle for all three, but as the Father rebuked them, here was the Son, and He is the one we must now listen to. Then, when they looked up they saw no one but Jesus, and when we look up to see as we should, we too will see no one but Jesus. We honor the Old Covenant for what it accomplished, and we honor the prophets for preparing His way, but now that the Son has come, we follow Him.

Understanding Elijah

17:9-13: Elijah was the prophet who confronted the false prophets who were deceiving Israel and turned the people back to the Lord. He also confronted the wayward government, and according to Malachi 4, will come to return the hearts of the fathers to the children and the hearts of the children to the fathers so that the Lord does not have to smite the land with a curse. John the Baptist did this to prepare the way for the Lord the first time He came. This is also the ministry that comes to prepare the way for the Lord at the end of the age. One of the important ways that we prepare the way for the Lord is to turn fathers to their children and children to their fathers.

Casting Out Demons

17:14-23: We see here that it takes faith to cast out demons, but that some, which He refers to here as "this kind," also require prayer and fasting. This was a demon that brought insanity. However, the earlier manuscripts do not have verse 21 and there is a reasonable challenge that it should not be included.

When Jesus told His disciples about His coming crucifixion, they were understandably grieved, but His emphasis was on His resurrection, which if they understood they would have rejoiced. As often as the Lord talked to them about the cross, He must bear that they obviously did not understand it until after it happened. We too often do not understand the crosses we must bear until after we have passed through the death into resurrection in that circumstance.

Fishing for Taxes

17:24-27: Jesus did not avoid paying taxes, and neither should we.

NOTES

THE GOSPEL OF
MATTHEW
Matthew 18

Who Is the Greatest in the Kingdom?

1 Then the disciples came to Jesus, saying, "Who is the greatest in the kingdom of heaven?"

2 Jesus drew a little child to Himself and set him in the middle of them, saying,

3 "It is true that unless you are converted and become as little children, you will not enter into the kingdom of heaven.

4 "Whoever will therefore humble himself as this little child, he is the greatest in the kingdom of heaven.

5 "Whoever will receive one such little child in My name receives Me.

A Warning to Stumbling Blocks

6 "Whoever will offend one of these little ones that believes in Me, it would be better for him that a millstone were hung around his neck, and that he were drowned in the depths of the sea.

7 "Woe to the world because of its offenses! They must come, but woe to that man by whom the offense comes!

8 "Therefore, if your hand or your foot offends you, cut them off, and cast them away. It is better for you to enter into life crippled or maimed, rather than having two hands or two feet and to be cast into everlasting fire.

9 "If your eye offends you, pluck it out, and cast it away. It is better for you to enter into life with one eye, rather than having two eyes to be cast into hell fire.

10 "Take heed that you do not despise one of these little ones, because their angels in heaven always behold the face of My Father which is in heaven.

11 "The Son of Man came to save that which was lost.

12 "Do you think that if a man has a hundred sheep, and one of them goes astray, that he would not leave the ninety-nine, go into the mountains and seek the one that had gone astray?

13 "If he finds it, he would rejoice more over that one sheep than over the ninety-nine that did not go astray.

14 "Even so, it is not the will of your Father which is in heaven for even one of these little ones to perish.

How to Approach the Sinful

15 "For this reason, if your brother sins against you, go and address it to him in private. If he hears you, you have gained your brother.

16 "If he will not listen to you, then take with you one or two more, so that by the mouth of two or three witnesses every word may be confirmed.

17 "If he refuses to listen to them, then tell it to the church. If he refuses to hear the church, let him be to you as a heathen and a tax collector.

18 "Whatever you will bind on earth will be bound in heaven, and whatever you loose on earth will be loosed in heaven.

19 "I repeat, that if two of you on earth shall fully agree about anything that they shall ask, it will be done for them by My Father who is in heaven.

20 "For where two or three are united together in My name, I will be in the midst of them."

21 Then Peter came to Him, and asked, "Lord, how often shall my brother sin against me, and I forgive him? Seven times?"

22 Jesus said to him, "I say to you, not just seven times, but seventy times seven.

Forgiveness

23 "Therefore the kingdom of heaven is like a certain king who wanted to settle the accounts of his servants.

24 "When he had begun to do this, one was brought to him which owed him ten million dollars.

25 "When he had nothing to pay, his lord commanded him to be sold, along with his wife and children, and all that he had, so that payment could to be made.

26 "The servant therefore fell down, and humbled himself, saying, 'Lord, have patience with me. I will pay you everything I owe.'

27 "Then the lord of that servant was moved with compassion and released him and forgave him the debt.

28 "Then this same servant went out and found one of his fellow servants who owed him two hundred dollars, and he grabbed him and took him by the throat, saying, 'Pay me what you owe me!'

29 "His fellow servant fell down at his feet and begged him, saying, 'Have patience with me, and I will pay you all that I owe.'

30 "But he refused, and instead had him cast into prison until he paid the debt.

31 "So when his fellow servants saw what he had done, they were grieved and came and told their lord everything that had happened.

32 "Then his lord called him and said, 'You wicked servant! I forgave you all of your huge debt because you entreated me!

33 "'Should you not have also had compassion on your fellow servant, even as I had mercy on you?'

34 "So his lord was very angry and delivered him to the tormentors until he paid all that was due.

35 "This is likewise what My heavenly Father will do to you if you do not forgive your brother that trespasses against you, from your heart."

Who Is the Greatest in the Kingdom?

Matthew 18-1-5: The characteristic of little children is humility, and we must have it to enter the kingdom. It is defined here as being teachable.

A Warning to Stumbling Blocks

18:6-14: Here the Lord's special love for children is apparent. Even among the worse criminals, crimes against children are especially heinous. With our own children, we have an ultimate trust from God, and in every Christian there should be a deep devotion to protect and take care of God's little ones.

For this reason, we should consider that if we went on a journey and entrusted our children to someone to take care of them, and came back and they had not been fed, clothed, kept clean, or protected from danger, how would we feel toward those we have given such a trust? How does God feel toward the way we have handled this trust?

How to Approach the Sinful

18:15-22: The Lord just said that it would be better to die than to be a stumbling block to even one of His children, and then He gives us this procedure to keep from being a stumbling block: If we see someone in sin, we must go to them personally and privately, before telling anyone else. Only if they do not repent should it ever be told to someone else, and then only one person who can also go with us to help them. This is a key—through this whole procedure we should seek to help the one who has fallen. Only if they refuse the counsel of two should it then be told to the church, and even this is done in a redemptive way so that we can all help to restore the one who has fallen into sin.

Forgiveness

18:23-35: Forgiveness is not an option but is the most basic discipline of the true Christian life. We should count every opportunity that we have to forgive as a privilege and opportunity to be more conformed to the image of Christ by taking up our cross to follow Him. As we are also told here, if we do not forgive, we are the ones who will go into bondage.

NOTES

The Gospel of
MATTHEW
Matthew 19

Doctrine on Divorce

1 When Jesus finished these teachings, He departed from Galilee and came to the coasts of Judaea beyond Jordan.

2 A great multitude followed Him, and He healed them there.

3 The Pharisees also came to Him, tempting Him by asking, "Is it lawful for a man to send away his wife for any cause?"

4 He answered them, "Have you not read that in the beginning He made them male and female,

5 "and said, **'For this cause a man shall leave father and mother, and shall cleave to his wife, and the two shall be one flesh?'**

6 "Therefore they are no longer two, but one flesh. What therefore God has joined together let no man divide asunder."

7 Then they asked Him, "Why did Moses then command to give a certificate of divorce, and to put her away?"

8 He said to them, "Because of the hardness of your hearts Moses allowed you to divorce your wives, but from the beginning it was not intended to be this way.

9 "I say to you that whoever does send away his wife, except for the cause of adultery, and marries another, commits adultery. Whoever marries the one who was sent away without cause also commits adultery."

10 His disciples said to Him, "If this is the case, it is better not to marry."

11 He said to them, "All men cannot receive this saying, except for those to whom it has been granted.

12 "For there are some eunuchs who were born that way, and there are some who were made eunuchs by men. There are also eunuchs that have made themselves eunuchs for the sake of the kingdom of heaven. He that is able to receive it, let him receive it."

The Children Come to Him

13 Then little children were brought to Him so that He could lay His hands on them and pray, but the disciples rebuked those who were bringing them.

14 Jesus said, "Allow the little children to come! Do not forbid them to come to Me, for the kingdom of heaven is for such as these."

15 So He laid His hands on them and then departed.

Righteousness and Riches

16 Then one came and said to Him, "Good Master, what good thing shall I do that I may have eternal life?"

17 He replied to him, "Why do you call Me good? There is none good but One, that is, God. However, if you want to enter into life, keep the commandments."

18 He said to him, "Which ones?" Jesus said, **"You shall not murder. You shall not commit adultery. You shall not steal. You shall not bear false witness.**

19 **"Honor your father and your mother, and, You shall love your neighbor as yourself"** (Exodus 20:12-15).

20 The young man said to Him, "All of these things I have kept from my youth up. What do I still lack?"

21 Jesus said to him, "If you desire to be perfect, go and sell what you have and give it to the poor, and you will have treasure in heaven. Then come and follow Me."

22 When the young man heard this, he went away grieved because he was very wealthy.

23 Then Jesus said to His disciples, "Truly I say to you that it is hard for a rich man to enter the kingdom of heaven.

24 "It is easier for a camel to go through the eye of a needle than for a rich man to enter into the kingdom of God."

25 When His disciples heard this, they were amazed and began saying, "Who then can be saved?"

26 Jesus discerned their reasoning and said to them, "With men this is impossible, but with God all things are possible."

27 Then Peter spoke up and said to Him, "We have forsaken all to follow You. What will be our reward?"

28 Jesus said to them, "Truly I say to you that you who have followed Me, in the regeneration when the Son of Man will sit on the throne in His glory, you also will sit upon twelve thrones judging the twelve tribes of Israel.

29 "Everyone who has forsaken houses, or brothers, or sisters, or father, or mother, or wife, or children, or lands, for My name's sake, will receive a hundredfold what they have given up in this life, and will inherit everlasting life.

30 "Many who are first will be last; and the last will be first."

Doctrine on Divorce

Matthew 19:1-12: Since divorce is now one of the most devastating plagues in Western culture, this is a crucial teaching. However, inadequate translations of this may have been the cause of many who have departed from the church, and some even from the faith. Here we can only address this superficially, as to do this as it deserves would require a book, but the following are the principles we want to consider:

- **God established marriage and does not want men to destroy it.**
- **God hates divorce.**
- **Divorce is the result of a hardness of heart.**
- **The law permits divorce for more liberal conditions than the Lord states here, which is why the Pharisees asked if it were permissible for "any reason." The Lord's answer therefore seemingly changes the law.**

- We know the Lord did not change the law because He asserted that He did not come to do this, but to fulfill it. Whenever there is such a conflict, it is almost always because of the translation, not what was actually said.
- The Scriptures never contradict when translated properly.

There are Greek scholars who assert that the typical English translation of this text is misleading. The Greek word for "divorce," which was a legal term, was not used here, though many English translations use "divorce" when it should have been translated "send away." A historical study of those times gives more insight into what the Lord was actually saying.

In the first century, the Pharisees were sending away their wives for just about anything, even for not being a good cook. They were justifying this because the Law of Moses specified that a man could send his wife away and give her a certificate of divorce if he found "any indecency" in her. As legalists are prone to do, they are strict with everyone else, but take extreme liberties when justifying what they want to do. However, in the first century they were sending their wives away without giving them a certificate of divorce that would free them to remarry. Without the certificate of divorce, any who remarried were committing adultery because they were still legally married.

Some who admit that this is the correct translation in this text also argue that to translate this as it should have been would only open the door wider for more divorce. That is an understandable concern, but the Word of God, translated as He intended, is always what we should seek. Obviously, what we are doing in regard to marriage and divorce is not working with about 50 percent of Christian marriages which are now ending in divorce. The following is a possible solution.

When I discussed this with an Orthodox Jewish rabbi to confirm these facts about the Pharisees, and to ask how they maintain such a low divorce rate in their community (about 6 percent), I was quite surprised by the answer, but quickly saw its brilliance and its Godly biblical wisdom. His answer was, they have such a low divorce rate because they have to allow divorce since it is in the Law of Moses. However, the divorce must be granted by a rabbi who takes them through the procedure for divorce, which is designed to find any way possible for reconciliation.

For example, they review the biblical curses that come upon anyone who breaks their vows, as well as things like the statistics of how children are affected when their parents divorce. They do this because they feel responsible to share with the couple the likely consequences of their actions. Most of the time they are able to preserve the marriage.

By not allowing divorce, Christian churches cannot take advantage of such a brilliant strategy, but instead Christians have to go before unbelieving judges for their divorce, usually using unbelieving lawyers. The result has been what Paul wrote to the Corinthians as one of the primary things that brought shame on the church (see I Corinthians 6).

Without question, the divorce rate among Christians at this time is one of the primary issues bringing shame on the name of Christ, and even though this is addressed very superficially here, this issue must be addressed and must be resolved with sound, biblical truth. It is my own opinion that the ultimate answer to this is to obey the two great commandments—to love God above all things and to love one another. As Jesus also taught, love is the fulfillment of the law. If we truly love God above all, including ourselves, we would endure just about anything for His name's sake, and certainly would be devoted to working out our marital problems to keep from doing what He hates. If we love one another as we are called to, then most of what causes divorce would not have a chance to get into our relationships, and we would love our children and others too much to injure them the way that divorce injures others. Ultimately, obeying the commandment to love is the answer.

Even so, there are cases where the safety of a spouse or the children requires a divorce. There are cases of unfaithfulness that also demand it. In these cases, one partner may be completely innocent, and to condemn them and their children to never again be married or to have a whole family is certainly not right, and is not what the Lord taught here or anywhere else in the Scriptures.

In summary, because Jesus Himself said that He did not come to change the law, and the law allowed for divorce under conditions other than adultery (see Deuteronomy 24:1-4), Jesus did not make a new law here. Neither does He say that if a divorced person remarries they are committing adultery. He was saying that one who "sent away" his wife, implying this is done without giving a certificate of divorce, they are committing adultery.

The Children Come to Him

19:13-15: The Lord loves children and wants them to come to Him. Possibly the biggest mistake many churches make is to babysit the children so the adults can be taught when some of the most important character traits of children are set by the time they are four years old. Their love for God and devotion to Him can already be set on a strong foundation by then. Because it is in the mouths of infants that "perfect praise" comes (see Psalm 8:2), children can touch God's heart in a special way.

Righteousness and Riches

19:16-30: The devotion to gaining and keeping our possessions is one of the primary things that keep people from the kingdom. Yet studies have shown that our possessions have practically no affect on our happiness. The happiest people in the world are those who have the most simple lives and strong relationships. Therefore, the kingdom is not only the door to eternal life but also the greatest joy in this life. A true kingdom life will be one of moderation, and mostly devoted to relationships. We are also promised that all who give up the things of this world to serve the King and His kingdom receive many times more than they gave up in this life, as well as unfathomable spiritual riches that will last forever.

NOTES

THE GOSPEL OF
MATTHEW
Matthew 20

The Reward of the Harvesters

1 "For the kingdom of heaven is like a landowner who went out early in the morning to hire laborers for his vineyard.

2 "When he had agreed with the laborers for a penny a day as their wages, he sent them into his vineyard.

3 "Again, he went out about the third hour and saw others standing idle in the marketplace,

4 "and said to them, 'You also go into the vineyard, and I will pay you what is fair.' So they went.

5 "Again he went out about the sixth and ninth hour and did the same thing.

6 "At the eleventh hour he went out and found others still standing idle and said to them, 'Why do you stand here idle all day?'

7 "They said to him, 'Because no one has hired us.' He said to them, 'You also go into the vineyard, and you will receive what is fair.'

8 "So when evening had come, the lord of the vineyard said to his steward, 'Call the laborers, and give them their wages, beginning with the last to come.'

9 "When those who were hired at the eleventh hour came, they each received a penny.

10 "But when the first came, they were therefore expecting to receive more, but they also received a penny each.

11 "So when they had received it, they grumbled against the good man of the house,

12 saying, 'These who were the last to come have worked but one hour, and you have made them equal to us who have borne the burden and heat of the day.'

13 "But he answered them, and said, 'Friends, I have done you no wrong. Did you not agree with me for a penny?'

14 'Take what is yours and go your way. If I give to the last the same as you,

15 'Is it not lawful for me to do what I will with my own? Is your eye evil because I am generous?'

16 "So the last shall be first, and the first last. For many are called, but few chosen."

Turning Toward Jerusalem

17 Jesus then departed for Jerusalem, and took the twelve disciples aside on the way and said to them,

18 "We are going to Jerusalem, and the Son of Man will be betrayed to the chief priests and to the scribes, and they will condemn Him to death,

19 "and will deliver Him to the Gentiles to mock and to scourge and to crucify Him, but on the third day He will rise again."

Authority in the Kingdom

20 "Then the mother of Zebedee's children came to Him with her sons, worshiping Him, and desiring a certain thing from Him.

21 So He said to her, "What is your request?" She said to Him, "Grant that these two sons of mine may sit on Your right hand, and on Your left in Your kingdom."

22 Jesus said to them, "You do not know what you ask. Are you able to drink of the cup that I will drink of? Are you able to be baptized with the baptism that I am baptized with?" They said to Him, "We are able."

23 Then He said to them, "You will indeed drink of My cup, and be baptized with the baptism that I am baptized with. However, to sit on My right hand and on My left is not Mine to give, but it will be given to the ones for whom it has been prepared by My Father."

24 When the other ten heard about this, they became indignant with the two brothers.

25 So Jesus called them to Himself, and said, "You know that the princes of the Gentiles exercise their authority to dominate and use others, and the greater their authority the more they use it for their own purposes.

26 "This must not be so among you. Whoever will be great among you will be your servant.

27 "Whoever will be greatest among you will be the greatest servant, the servant of all,

28 "just as the Son of Man did not come to be served, but to serve, and to give His life a ransom for many."

Healing the Two Blind Men

29 As they departed from Jericho, a great multitude followed Him.

30 Two blind men sitting by the wayside heard that Jesus was passing by and cried out, saying, "Have mercy on us, O Lord, Son of David."

31 The multitude rebuked them, telling them to be quiet, but they cried even louder, saying, "Have mercy on us, O Lord, Son of David!"

32 Then Jesus stood still and called them, and said, "What do you want Me to do for you?"

33 They said to Him, "Lord, we ask for our eyes to be opened."

34 So Jesus had compassion on them, and touched their eyes, and immediately they received their sight and followed Him.

The Reward of the Harvesters

Matthew 20:1-16: We should always rejoice in the generosity of the Lord whether it is to us or to others.

Turning Toward Jerusalem

20:17-19: The Lord knew what would happen to Him in Jerusalem, but never drew back from the cross He had been

given to bear. It was to be one of the most tragic and triumphant events in history, and His reward would be the world. We too will always have a reward that is more than worth the cross that we must bear if we will take it up.

Authority in the Kingdom

20:20-28: In this present world, promotion usually goes to the self-seeking and self-promoting, but the kingdom promotion will go to those who are best at promoting and serving others. Which kingdom are we now serving?

Healing the Two Blind Men

20:29-34: We do not have an example in any of the Gospels of Jesus refusing to heal any who came to Him. He has not changed. Sometimes it took extraordinary faith and perseverance for them to get to Him, but those who persevered always received what they asked for.

NOTES

THE GOSPEL OF
MATTHEW
Matthew 21

The Triumphal Entry

1 When they drew close to Jerusalem, at Bethphage on the Mount of Olives, Jesus sent two disciples,

2 saying to them, "Go into that village, and you will find a donkey tied, and a colt with her. Loose them, and bring them to Me.

3 "If any one says anything to you tell them, 'The Lord has need of them,' and he will send them."

4 All this was done so that it would be fulfilled which was spoken by the prophet, saying,

5 **"Tell the daughter of Zion, 'Behold, your King comes to you in humility, sitting upon a donkey, a colt, the foal of a donkey"** (Isaiah 62:11; Zechariah 9:9).

6 So the disciples went and did as Jesus had commanded them,

7 and brought the donkey and the colt, laid their garments on them, and then set Him upon it.

8 A very great multitude spread their garments on the road. Others cut down branches from the trees and laid them in the way.

9 The multitudes that went before, and those who followed, all cried out, saying, "Hosanna to the Son of David! Blessed is He who comes in the name of the Lord! Hosanna in the highest."

10 So when He had come into Jerusalem, the whole city was stirred, saying, "Who is this?"

11 The multitude answered, saying, "This is Jesus the Prophet, from Nazareth of Galilee."

Cleansing the Temple

12 Jesus went into the temple of God, and cast out all who bought and sold in the temple, and tipped over the tables of the moneychangers and the seats of those who sold doves,

13 saying to them, "It is written, **'My house shall be called the house of prayer'** (Isaiah 56:7; Jeremiah 7:11), but you have made it a den of thieves!'"

14 Then the blind and the lame came to Him in the temple, and He healed them.

15 When the chief priests and scribes saw the wonderful things that He did, and the children crying out in the temple, and saying, "Hosanna to the Son of David," they were outraged.

16 So they said to Him, "Do you not hear what they are saying?" Jesus replied, "Yes. Have you never read, **'Out of the mouth of babes and infants praise is perfected?"** (Psalm 8:2).

17 So He left them and went out of the city to lodge at Bethany.

Cursing the Fig Tree

18 The next morning as He returned to the city, He was hungry,

19 and when He saw a fig tree on the way, He went up to it and found nothing on it but leaves. Then He said to it, "Let no fruit grow on you again, forever." Immediately the fig tree withered away.

20 When the disciples saw this they marveled, saying, "How quickly the fig tree withered away!"

21 Jesus then said to them, "Truly I say to you, if you have faith and do not doubt, you will not only do what was done to the fig tree, but if you will say to this mountain, 'Be removed, and be cast into the sea,' it will be done.

22 "All things that you will ask in prayer, believing, you will receive."

The Basis of His Authority

23 When He had come into the temple, the chief priests and the elders of the people came to Him as He was teaching and said, "By what authority do You do these things? Who gave You this authority?"

24 Jesus answered them, "I will ask you one question, which if you tell Me I will likewise tell you by what authority I do these things.

25 "The baptism of John, where did it come from? Was it from heaven or from man?" They reasoned among themselves, saying, "If we say, 'From heaven,' He will say to us, 'Then why did you not believe him?'

26 "If we say, 'From man,' we fear the people because they all hold John to be a prophet."

27 So they answered Jesus and said, "We do not know." So He said to them, "Neither will I tell you by what authority I do these things.

Parable of the Obedient Son

28 "What do you think? A certain man had two sons, and he came to the first and said, 'Son, go work today in my vineyard.'

29 "He answered and said, 'I will not,' but afterward he repented and went.

30 "So he came to the second, and said likewise. This son answered and said, 'I will go, sir,' but he did not go.

31 "Which of the two did the will of his father?" They said to Him, "The first." Jesus said to them, "Truly I say to you that the tax collectors and harlots will enter the kingdom of God before you.

32 "For John came to you in the way of righteousness, and you did not believe him, but the tax collectors and harlots believed him. When you saw it you still did not repent that you might believe him."

Parable of the Unrighteous Husbandman

33 "Hear another parable: There was a landowner who planted a vineyard and hedged it all around, and dug a winepress in it, and built a tower. Then he leased it out to husbandmen and went into a far country.

34 "When the time of the fruit drew near, he sent his servants to the husbandmen so that they might receive the fruit of it.

35 "The husbandmen took his servants, and beat one, and killed another, and stoned the third.

36 "Again, he sent even more servants than at first, and they did the same to them.

37 "Last of all he sent to them his son, saying, 'They will respect my son.'

38 "When the husbandmen saw the son, they said to one another, 'This is the heir. Come, let us kill him and let us seize his inheritance.'

39 "They caught him, and cast him out of the vineyard and slew him.

40 "When the lord therefore of the vineyard comes, what will he do to those husbandmen?"

41 They said to Him, "He will destroy those miserable wicked men, and will lease out his vineyard to other husbandmen, which will pay him what is owed at the right time."

42 Jesus said to them, "Did you never read in the Scripture, **'The stone that the builders rejected, the same has become the head cornerstone: this is the Lord's doing, and it is marvelous in our eyes?'** (Psalm 18:22-23)

43 "Therefore I say to you, the kingdom of God will be taken from you and given to a people who will bring forth the fruit of it.

44 "Whosoever will fall on this stone will be broken, but on whomever it will fall it will grind him to powder."

45 When the chief priests and Pharisees heard His parables, they perceived that He spoke of them,

46 but when they tried to seize Him, they feared the multitude, because they considered Him to be a prophet.

The Triumphal Entry

Matthew 21:1-11: The triumphal entry Jesus made to Jerusalem was certainly a wonderful thing. The multitude was acknowledging Jesus as their King and as the One who had fulfilled the prophecies of the coming Messiah. Even so, in just five days the same multitude would be crying out "Crucify Him!" This is the danger of raising up great congregations who are not disciples and have their own relationship to Him. Groups can be easily manipulated as the up and down swings of pub-

lic opinion polls reveal. However, those who have a personal relationship to Him will not be so easily shaken or misled.

Cleansing the Temple

21:12-17: The first thing Jesus did was to clean the merchants out of the temple, and then He healed the sick. Healing people is also cleansing for His house.

Cursing the Fig Tree

21:18-22: The Lord expects fruit from us as well. Those who are not bearing fruit are not abiding in Him as we read in John 15. Those who claim to be His but do not bear fruit are not really joined to Him, and therefore, they too will be cut off.

In Isaiah 60, we see that at the time of deep darkness we will also see the glory of the Lord. In these times of great doubt and skepticism, we will also see some of the greatest demonstrations of faith, including mountains being moved.

The Basis of His Authority

21:23-27: When Jesus was asked by what authority He did His works, He was not deflecting their question by asking them where the baptism of John had come from. The answer to His question was the answer to their question. Jesus had credentials like no one else in history. Prophets had foretold of His coming for thousands of years, and John was there as their representative to say that Jesus was the One they had all prepared the way for. If you understand John, you will understand Jesus.

Parable of the Obedient Son

21:28-32: Those who tend to be the most faithful and obedient to the Lord are usually those who have been through rebellion, saying they would not obey Him, but then returned to Him. We must not give up on those who go astray for a time.

Parable of Unrighteous Husbandman

21:33-46: This remarkable parable perfectly fit what was happening with Israel, and the leaders of Israel saw it, and still did what they said should have gotten the wicked husbandmen destroyed. The hardness of heart that fallen men can have is truly remarkable.

NOTES

THE GOSPEL OF
MATTHEW
Matthew 22

Parable of the Wedding Feast

1 Jesus continued to speak to them in parables and said,

2 "The kingdom of heaven is like a certain king who arranged a marriage for his son,

3 "He then sent his servants to call those who were invited to the wedding, but they would not come.

4 "Again, he sent his servants, saying, 'Tell the ones who were invited, 'Behold, I have prepared my dinner, my oxen and my fatlings have been killed, and everything is ready. Come to the marriage.'

5 "Instead they made light of it and went their own ways, one to his farm, another to his merchandise.

6 "The remaining ones took his servants, and treated them spitefully, and slew them.

7 "When the king heard of it, he was enraged, and he sent forth his armies, and destroyed those murderers and burned up their city.

8 "Then he said to his servants, 'The wedding is ready, but the ones who were invited were not worthy.

9 "'Go therefore into the highways, and as many as you will find invite to the marriage.'

10 "So those servants went out into the highways and gathered together as many as they found, both bad and good, and the wedding was filled with guests.

11 "When the king came in to see the guests, he saw a man who did not have on a wedding garment,

12 "and he said to him, 'Friend, how did you come here without wearing a wedding garment?' He could not answer.

13 "Then the king said to the servants, 'Bind him hand and foot, take him away, and cast him into outer darkness where there will be weeping and gnashing of teeth.'

14 "Many are called, but few are chosen."

Paying Tribute to Caesar

15 Then the Pharisees planned a way to ensnare Him in His teaching.

16 So they sent their disciples out to Him with the Herodians, saying, "Master, we know that You are true, and teach the way of God in truth. Neither do You fear any man, for You do not regard the status of men.

17 "Tell us therefore, What do You think? Is it lawful to give tribute to Caesar, or not?"

18 Jesus perceived their treachery, and said, "Why do you temp Me, you hypocrites?

19 "Show Me the tribute money." So they brought to Him a penny.

20 He said to them, "Whose inscription and image is this?"

21 They answered Him, "Caesar's." Then He said to them, "Render to Caesar the things that are Caesar's and to God the things that are God's."

22 When they heard His answer they marveled, and left Him alone, going their own way.

Marriage in the Resurrection

23 The same day the Sadducees, who do not believe in a resurrection, came to Him and asked,

24 "Master, Moses said, 'If a man dies, having no children, his brother is to marry his wife, and raise up children in the name of his brother.

25 "Now there were seven brothers, and the first, when he had married a wife, died, and having no children, left his wife to his brother.'

26 "The same happened to the second also, and the third, all the way to the seventh.

27 "Last of all the woman died.

28 "In the resurrection, whose wife will she be? Which of the seven? For they all had her."

29 Jesus answered and said to them, "You do err, not knowing the Scriptures or the power of God.

30 "For in the resurrection they will neither marry, nor are given in marriage, but are like the angels of God in heaven.

31 "But concerning the resurrection of the dead, have you not read that which was spoken to you by God, saying,

32 "**'I am the God of Abraham, and the God of Isaac, and the God of Jacob?'** (Exodus 3:6) God is not the God of the dead, but of the living."

33 When the multitude heard this, they were astonished at His teaching.

34 When the Pharisees heard that He had silenced the Sadducees, they gathered to challenge Him.

The Greatest Commandment

35 Then one of them, which was a lawyer, asked Him a question to tempt Him, saying,

36 "Master, which is the greatest commandment in the law?"

37 Jesus said to him, "**'You shall love the Lord your God with all of your heart, and with all of your soul, and with all of your mind'** (Deuteronomy 6:5).

38 "This is the first and great commandment.

39 "The second is like it, **'You shall love your neighbor as yourself'** (Leviticus 19:18).

40 "It is on these two commandments that the law and the prophets are established."

41 While the Pharisees were gathered, Jesus asked them a question,

The Son of David

42 saying, "What do you think concerning the Christ? Whose Son is He? They said to Him, "The Son of David."

43 He said to them, "How then does David call Him Lord in the Spirit, saying,

44 **'The Lord said to my Lord, "Sit at My right hand until I make Your enemies Your footstool?"'** (Psalm 110:1)

45 "If David then called Him Lord, how is He his Son?"

46 No one was able to answer Him anything. Neither did any man ask Him any more questions from that time on.

Parable of the Wedding Feast

Matthew 22:1-14: This parable accurately foretold how the messengers of the Lord have been treated. Even so, the Lord will have a wedding for His Son, and those who celebrate with Him will be a great host.

This also illustrates the importance of dressing appropriately for occasions. How we dress for an occasion indicates our level of respect for to occasion and for the host.

Paying Tribute to Caesar

22:15-22: Even though we are citizens of the kingdom, we are also citizens of the nations that we have been placed in to be salt and light. We therefore pay taxes just as Jesus taught here.

Marriage in the Resurrection

22:23-34: The details of our heavenly nature are few and often ambiguous in Scripture as we are told just what we now need to know. Even so, from what we are told, it will be glorious beyond our present finite minds, and we just cannot relate it very well to the things of this world.

God has not related differently to the different generations, but He is the same with all.

In verse 29, we see one of the primary reasons that so many fall into error: Those who know the Scriptures but do not know His power will often fall to the error of legalism.

Those who know the power but do not know the Scriptures will fall to the error of lawlessness. We must be devoted to knowing His Word and His power if we are going to stay on the path of life.

The Greatest Commandment

22:35-41: Love is the basic answer to everything we are called to be and to do.

The Son of David

22:42-46: The religious leaders of the time asked Jesus a multitude of questions and could never stump Him, but He just asked them one and they could not answer it. Religion without God is a pitiful thing.

NOTES

THE GOSPEL OF
MATTHEW
Matthew 23

Rebuke for the Scribes and Pharisees

1 Then Jesus spoke to the multitude and to His disciples,

2 saying, "The scribes and the Pharisees sit in Moses' seat.

3 "Therefore do whatever they tell you to do, but do not do what they do, because they command others what they do not do themselves.

4 "For they bind heavy burdens on men's shoulders, but they themselves will not move even a finger to lift them.

5 "All their works they do to be seen by men. They make their phylacteries broad, and enlarge the borders of their garments,

6 "and love the highest places at feasts, and the chief seats in the synagogues,

7 "and greetings in the markets, and to be called by men, 'Rabbi, Rabbi.'

Kingdom Authority

8 "However, you are not to be called Rabbi, for one is your Teacher, even Christ, and all of you are brethren.

9 "Call no man on earth your father, because One is your Father, Who is in heaven.

10 "Neither be called 'masters,' because one is your Master, even Christ.

11 "He that is the greatest among you will be your servant.

12 "Whoever will exalt himself will be humbled, and he that will humble himself will be exalted.

Condemnation for the Scribes and Pharisees

13 "Woe to you, scribes and Pharisees—you are hypocrites! You shut up the kingdom of heaven to keep men from entering. You do not enter in yourselves, or allow those who are desiring to enter.

14 "Woe to you, scribes and Pharisees because you are hypocrites! For you devour widows' houses, and for a pretense make long prayers. Therefore you will receive the greater condemnation.

15 "Woe to you, scribes and Pharisees—hypocrites! You compass sea and land to make one disciple, and when he is made, you make him twice the child of hell that you are yourselves.

16 "Woe to you, you blind guides! You say, 'Whoever will swear by the temple is not obligated, but whoever swears by the gold of the temple, he is obligated!'

17 "You fools—you are blind! For what is greater, the gold or the temple that sanctifies the gold?

18 "*You say,* 'If you swear by the altar, it is nothing, but whoever swears by the gift that is upon it, he is obligated.'

19 "You blind fools! For what is greater, the gift or the altar that sanctifies the gift?

20 "Therefore, whosoever will swear by the altar, swears by it, and by all things that are on it.

21 "Whosoever will swear by the temple, swears by it, and by Him who dwells therein.

22 "He that will swear by heaven swears by the throne of God, and by Him that sits on it.

23 "Woe to you, scribes and Pharisees—hypocrites! For you pay tithes of mint, anise, and cummin, and have omitted the weightier matters of the law which are: justice, mercy, and faith. These are the things you should have done, while not leaving the other things undone.

24 "You blind guides! You strain at a gnat and swallow a camel.

25 "Woe to you, scribes and Pharisees—hypocrites! For you clean

the outside of the cup and the platter, but within they are full of extortion and excess.

26 "You blind Pharisees! Clean the inside of the cup and platter first, then the outside may be clean also.

27 "Woe to you, scribes and Pharisees—hypocrites! For you are like whitewashed tombs, which indeed appear beautiful on the outside, but on the inside are full of dead men's bones and of all kinds of uncleanness.

28 "Just like them you also appear outwardly righteous to men, but within you are full of hypocrisy and lawlessness.

29 "Woe to you, scribes, Pharisees—hypocrites! Because you build the tombs of the prophets and beautify the tombs of the righteous,

30 "and say, 'If we had lived in the days of our fathers, we would not have been partakers with them in shedding the blood of the prophets.'

31 "Therefore, you are witnesses against yourselves, that you are indeed the children of those who killed the prophets.

32 "You will be measured with your fathers.

33 "You serpents, you generation of vipers! How can you escape the judgment of Gehenna?

34 "Therefore, I will send to you prophets, wise men, and scribes, and some of them you will kill and crucify, and some of them you will scourge in your synagogues and persecute from city to city.

35 "By this it will be proven that you are the same as those who shed all the righteous blood shed upon the earth, from the blood of righteous Abel to the blood of Zacharias son of Barachiah, whom you slew between the temple and the altar.

36 "Truly I say to you, all these things will come upon this generation.

Lament for Jerusalem

37 "O Jerusalem, Jerusalem, that kills the prophets and stones those who are sent to you. How often would I have gathered your children together like a hen gathers her chicks under her wings, but you would not come!

38 "Behold, your house is left to you desolate.

39 "For I say to you that you will not see Me from this time forth until you shall say, 'Blessed is he that comes in the name of the Lord.'"

Rebuke for the Scribes and Pharisees

Chapter 23:1-7: This is a clear warning from the Lord to watch out for those who love titles and appearances. Such ministries will likewise result in the superficial devotion to religious performance rather than the path of life, which is growing in love for God and one another, living the life of the cross which is sacrifice, and considering ourselves as servants.

Kingdom Authority

23:8-12: Those who have kingdom authority will not be found promoting themselves trying to be recognized. These have an understanding that God resists the proud but gives His grace to the humble, and there is nothing that we need more than His grace. The true also know that everyone who promotes and exalts himself will be humbled. The true are those who seek the lowest place and become the servants of others.

Condemnation for the Scribes and Pharisees

23:9-36: One of the great revelations of the heart of God is how much mercy He had for sinners, and how little tolerance He had for the self-righteous. He has not changed.
Lament for Jerusalem

23:37-39: The second worst judgment in Scripture came upon Jerusalem because they did not know the time of their visitation. When we do not see Him when He comes, it is because we are not looking for Him, and have our main attention upon something else.

If we are going to see Him now, we must see Him in those He sends to us. How often do we miss Him like the two men on the Road to Emmaus because He appears to us in a form we are not familiar with? If they had known Him after the

Spirit instead of after appearances, they would have recognized Him. Do we know Him after the Spirit?

NOTES

THE GOSPEL OF
MATTHEW
Matthew 24

The End of the Temple Prophesied

1 Then Jesus departed from the temple, and His disciples came to show Him the buildings of the temple.

2 Jesus then said to them, "Do you see all these things? Truly I say to you that there will not be one stone left upon another, but every one of them will be thrown down."

Signs of the End of the Age

3 Then as He sat on the Mount of Olives, the disciples came to Him privately and asked, "Tell us, when will these things come to pass? What will be the sign of Your coming and of the end of the age?"

4 So Jesus answered and said to them, "Take heed that no one deceives you.

5 "For many will come in My name, saying that I am the Christ, and yet they will deceive many.

6 "You will hear of wars and rumors of wars. See that you are not disturbed, but keep your peace. All of these things must come to pass, but that is not yet the end.

7 "For there will be ethnic wars, and kingdoms rising against kingdoms. There shall be famines, and pestilence, and earthquakes in many different places.

8 "All these are but the beginning of sorrows.

9 "Then they will deliver you up to be afflicted and will kill you, and you will be hated in all nations for My name's sake.

10 "During that time even many of My disciples will become of-fended, and will betray one another, and even hate one another.

11 "Many false prophets will arise and will deceive many.

12 "Because lawlessness will spread, the love of many will grow cold.

13 "He who endures to the end will be saved.

14 "This gospel of the kingdom will be preached in all the world for a witness to all nations, and then will the end come.

15 "Therefore, when you see the abomination of desolation that was spoken of by Daniel the prophet standing in the holy place (let him who reads understand),

16 then let those who are in Judea flee into the mountains.

17 "Let him who is on the housetop not come down to take anything out of his house.

18 "Neither let him who is in the field return back to get his clothes.

19 "Woe to those who are with child and to those that nurse babes in those days!

20 "Pray that your flight will not be in the winter or on the Sabbath day,

21 because there will be tribulation at that time such as there has not been since the beginning of the world to this time, nor will there ever be such tribulation again.

22 "Except those days are shortened, no one would survive them, but for the elect's sake those days will be shortened.

23 "Then, if any man will say to you, 'Look! Here is the Christ,' or 'There He is,' do not believe it.

24 "For false christs and false prophets will arise and will demonstrate great signs and wonders so that if it were possible they would deceive even the elect.

25 "Behold, I have told you this before it happens.

26 "Therefore, if they say to you, 'Behold, He is in the desert,' do not go. Or if they should say, 'He is in the secret chambers,' do not believe it.

27 "For as the sun comes out of the east and spreads across the sky even to the west, so will the coming of the Son of Man be.

28 "For wherever the body is, there will the eagles be gathered together.

29 "Immediately after the tribulation of those days the sun will be darkened, and the moon will not give her light, and the stars will fall from heaven, and the powers of the heavens will be shaken.

30 "Then the sign of the Son of Man will appear in heaven, and all of the tribes of the earth will mourn when they see the Son of Man coming in the clouds of heaven with power and great glory.

31 "He will send forth His angels with the sound of a great trumpet, and they will gather together His elect from the four winds, from one end of heaven to the other.

32 "Now you must learn a parable about the fig tree. When its branch is still tender and it puts forth leaves, you know that summer is close.

33 "So likewise, when you see all of these things, know that the time is near, even at the door.

34 "Truly I say to you, this generation will not pass until all of these things are fulfilled.

35 "Heaven and earth will pass away, but My words will not pass away.

36 "However, no one knows the day or the hour, nor do the angels in heaven, but My Father alone.

37 "It will be like the times of Noah when the Son of Man comes.

38 "For as in the days that were before the flood, they were eating and drinking, marrying and giving in marriage, until the day that Noah entered into the ark,

39 and they did not understand what was happening until the flood came and took them all away, so will the coming of the Son of Man be.

40 "As two are in the field, one will be taken and the other left.

41 "Two women will be grinding at the mill, and one will be taken while the other one is left.

42 "Watch therefore, and be on the alert, for you do not know what hour your Lord is coming.

43 "Understand this: If the good man of the house had known in

what watch the thief would come, he would have been awake and would not have allowed his house to be broken into.

44 "Therefore, you also be ready, for at a time when you are not expecting, the Son of Man will come.

45 "Who then is a faithful and wise servant, who his Lord has made ruler over his household to give them their food at the proper time?

46 "Blessed is that servant whom, when his Lord comes, will find him so doing.

47 "Truly I say to you, He will make him ruler over all of His possessions.

48 "If that evil servant shall say in his heart, 'My Lord delays His coming,'

49 and will begin to beat his fellow servants, and to eat and drink with the drunken,

50 the Lord of that servant will come in a day when he is not looking for Him, and in an hour that he is not aware,

51 and will cut him down, and appoint him his portion with the hypocrites, where there shall be weeping and gnashing of teeth."

The End of the Temple Prophesied

Matthew 24:1-2: In the Lord's discourse, He made a distinction between "their" temple and "His" temple. The temple of man cannot last, but the temple of the Lord will last forever. Which are we building?

Signs of the End of the Age

24:3-51: The first thing the Lord said about the end of the age was not to be deceived. Here He gives clear and specific warnings of those things that would deceive.

First, He warned that many would come in His name declaring that He indeed was the Christ, but would still be deceivers. History is full of these, and there are many today. It is not enough for one to acknowledge Jesus is the Christ for them to be true teachers. We must confirm their message with the Scriptures, and examine the fruit of what they teach.

Verse 12: When He warns that the love of many will grow cold, He is speaking of Christians because non-Christians do not have a love for Him that can grow cold. Note that this happens because of lawlessness. In Romans 6:19, we see that lawlessness is the result of impurity, which are things like pornography and other lusts of the flesh that result in the defilement of our bodies. These things will kill our love for God and lead to being a part of this most unhappy group who fell away from Him at the end.

Verse 14: The gospel of the kingdom has not been preached since the first century. We have preached the gospel of salvation and the gospel about many of the truths of God but not the gospel of His kingdom. This is a major sign we are waiting for, to see this gospel preached all over the world. It is the gospel, so it is good news, not bad news. It is not the message of the end of the world, but of a new beginning for the whole world.

Verse 19: We might interpret this "Woe to those who keep their people in immaturity."

Verse 22: If these days had to be shortened because no one would survive, and the elect had been raptured before these things, why would these days have to be shortened for their sake?

Verse 27: The word translated "coming" in this verse and verse 3 is the Greek *parousia*, which literally means "presence." The Greek word that is often translated "lightning" in this text could be translated "the sun." Lightning does not always come out of the east and go west, but the sun does. There are signs that the sun is about to rise, which are easy to discern, but you have to be awake early enough, and you have to be looking in the right direction to see them. Do you see them?

Verse 28: The eagles will be gathering where there is *spiritual* food. Sound teaching will always be a main attraction of the elect.

Verses 29-31: This is the rapture when His sign appears in the heavens at the end of this period. As we see here, it is then that He sends forth His angels to gather His elect.

Verses 32-34: The fig tree is the sign of Israel. The regathering of the Jewish people to their homeland is one of the important signs of the times. The word that is literally translated "generation" here is connected to genealogy, indicating that He is speaking more of the Jewish people not passing away being the promise. With nearly a thousand years in which there have been almost continuous attempts to wipe out this one people group, this is a great promise and a great sign. Whether it is the Philistines, the Hittites, or any of the other groups of this region, they have all disappeared but the Jewish people. Never before has a people group been driven from their homeland and survived. The Jewish people were separated from their homeland after 70 A.D., and not only maintained an identity for over 1800 years, but they returned to their homeland. This is unprecedented, and a great sign of God's power to keep us and to restore us.

Verse 36-44: It is ultimate foolishness to follow anyone who thinks they know the date Jesus will return. Much of the body of Christ was fooled by the "88 Reasons Why Christ Will Return in 1988." When this proved false, a huge number then succumbed to the "89 Reasons Christ Will Return in 1989," and to a number of other such follies. As the Lord makes clear here, NO ONE KNOWS THE DAY OR THE HOUR, not even the angels! We will know when it happens. The only thing we know is that He will come when we are not expecting Him to. Therefore, if so many are expecting a certain day, that can't be it.

Verses 45-51: The faithful servant will be faithfully giving food to His household when He comes. This is sound teaching. The unfaithful will get impatient and start to take advantage of God's people for their own gain.

NOTES

The Gospel of
MATTHEW
Matthew 25

The Wise and Foolish Virgins

1 "Then the kingdom of heaven will be compared to ten virgins who took their lamps and went to meet the bridegroom.

2 "Five of them were wise, and five were foolish.

3 "The ones who were foolish took their lamps but did not take any oil with them.

4 "The wise took oil in their vessels along with their lamps.

5 "While the bridegroom tarried, they all fell asleep.

6 "At midnight there was a cry, 'Behold, the bridegroom is coming. Go out to meet him!'

7 "Then all those virgins arose and trimmed their lamps.

8 "So the foolish said to the wise, 'Give us some of your oil, because our lamps have gone out.'

9 "But the wise answered, 'No! If we do that there will not be enough for us. Go to the merchants and buy your own.'

10 "While they had gone to buy the oil, the bridegroom came, and the ones who were ready went in with him to the marriage, and the door was shut.

11 "Afterward the other virgins also came, saying, 'Lord! Lord! Open to us!'

12 "He answered and said, 'Truly I say to you, I do not know you.'

13 "Watch therefore, for you do not know neither the day nor the hour when the Son of Man will come.

Parable of the Talents

14 "For the kingdom of heaven is like a man traveling to a far country who called his servants and delivered his goods to them.

15 "To one he gave five talents, to another two, and to another one, which were each according to his ability. He then left on his journey.

16 "The one who had received the five talents went and traded with them and made five more talents.

17 "Likewise, he who had received two gained another two.

18 "He who had received one went and buried his lord's money.

19 "After a long time the lord of those servants came and settled accounts with them.

20 "He who had received five talents came and brought the other five talents, saying, 'Lord, you delivered to me five talents, and I have gained five more.'

21 "His lord said to him, 'Well done! You are a good and faithful servant. You have been faithful over a few things, so I will make you ruler over many things. Enter into the joy of your lord.'

22 "Then the one who had received the two talents came and said, 'Lord, you gave me two talents, and see, I have gained two more talents beside them.'

23 "His lord said to him, 'Well done, good and faithful servant. You have been faithful over a few things, so I will make you a ruler over many things. Enter into the joy of your lord.'

24 "Then he who had received the one talent came and said, 'Lord, I know that you are a hard man, reaping where you have not sown, and gathering where you have not scattered seed.

25 'Therefore I was afraid, and went and hid your talent in the ground. So, here is what is yours.'

26 "His lord answered and said to him, 'You wicked, lazy slave! You knew that I reap where I have not sown, and gather where I have not scattered seed.

27 'You should have put my money in the bank, and then when I came I would have at least also received what I had with interest.

28 'Therefore take the talent from him, and give it to him who has the ten talents.

29 'For to every one who has will more be given, and he will have an abundance. From the one who does not have much, even what he has will be taken away.

30 'Cast the unprofitable servant into outer darkness. There will be weeping and gnashing of teeth.'

The Parable of the Sheep and Goats

31 "When the Son of Man comes in His glory, and all the holy angels are with Him, He will then sit on the throne in His glory.

32 "And they will gather all the nations before Him, and He will separate them like a shepherd separates his sheep from the goats.

33 "He will set the sheep on His right hand, but the goats on the left.

34 "Then the King will say to those on His right hand, 'Come, you blessed of My Father, inherit the kingdom prepared for you from the foundation of the world.

35 'Because I was a hungry, and you gave Me food. I was thirsty, and you gave Me drink. I was a stranger, and you took Me in;

36 naked, and you clothed Me. I was sick, and you visited Me. I was in prison, and you came to visit Me.'

37 "Then the righteous will answer Him, saying, 'Lord, when did we see You hungry and feed You? Or thirsty and give You a drink?

38 'When did we see You as a stranger and take You in? Or naked and clothe You?

39 'Or when did we see You sick, or in prison, and come to You?'

40 "The King will answer them, 'Truly I say to you, as you have done it to even one of the least of these My brethren, you have done it to Me.'

41 "Then He will say to those on the left hand, 'Depart from Me, you who are accursed into the everlasting fire prepared for the devil and his angels.

42 'I was hungry, and you did not give Me anything to eat. I was thirsty, and you did not give Me a drink.

43 'I was a stranger, and you did not take Me in; naked, and you did not clothe Me. I was sick and in prison, and you did not visit Me.'

44 "Then they will also answer Him, saying, 'Lord, when did we see You hungry, or thirsty, or a stranger, or naked, or sick, or in prison, and did not minister to You?'

45 "Then He will answer them, saying, 'Truly I say to you, as you did not do it to one of the least of these, you did not do it to Me.'

46 "These shall go into the eternal punishment, but the righteous into eternal life."

The Wise and Foolish Virgins

Matthew 25:1-13: Nothing is more important in our lives than staying close to the Lord and staying filled with the Holy Spirit. This is a basic lifestyle for the true disciple of Christ. Those who become lazy or distracted can pay a terrible price, but this is just if we do not esteem our calling to the King more than this.

Parable of the Talents

25:14-30: Talents were money. Though the Lord uses money in this parable, we can know that it has to do with all of the resources He has entrusted to us, spiritual and natural. It has been estimated that between one-third and one-half of the teachings on righteousness in Scripture have to do with stewardship—managing what has been entrusted to us. Here we see that this will be one of the key factors that will determine whether we hear, "Well done, good and faithful servant," or "you wicked evil slave" on that great Judgment Day.

The Parable of the Sheep and Goats

25:31-46: First, we see here that the Lord is going to divide the nations, not just individuals, as "sheep" or "goats." However, just because He speaks of the nations here, we should not assume that it does not apply to individuals too, for surely it does. If we think that it would be wonderful to be able to do something that would especially touch God's heart today, we can, just by doing something that would touch

even the least of His little ones. What do we have to do that is more important than this?

NOTES

THE GOSPEL OF
MATTHEW
Matthew 26

1 When Jesus had finished all these teachings, He said to His disciples,

2 "You know that after two days it is the Feast of the Passover, and the Son of Man will be betrayed to be crucified."

3 Then the chief priests, the scribes, and the elders of the people assembled together in the palace of the high priest, who was called Caiaphas.

4 There they consulted about how they might take Jesus by subtlety and kill Him.

5 Even so, they said, "Not on the feast day, lest there be an uproar among the people."

Anointed for Burial

6 At that time Jesus was in Bethany, in the house of Simon the leper,

7 and a woman having an alabaster box of very precious ointment came to Him and poured it on His head as He was eating.

8 When His disciples saw it, they were indignant, saying, "To what purpose is this waste?

9 "This ointment might have been sold for a lot of money that could have been given to the poor."

10 When Jesus heard them, He said, "Why are you troubling the woman? She has done a good thing for Me.

11 "For you will always have the poor with you, but you will not always have Me.

12 "For when she poured this ointment on My body, it was for My burial.

13 "Truly I say to you that wherever this gospel is preached in the whole world it will also be told what this woman has done as a memorial of her."

Betrayal and Denial

14 Then one of the twelve, Judas Iscariot, went to the chief priests,

15 and said to them, "What will you give me if I deliver Him to you?" They agreed to give him thirty pieces of silver.

16 From that time on he sought for an opportunity to betray Him.

17 On the first day of the Feast of Unleavened Bread, the disciples came to Jesus, saying, "Where do You want us to prepare for You to eat the Passover?"

18 He said, "Go into the city to a certain man, and say to him, 'The Master says, 'My time is at hand. I will keep the Passover at your house with My disciples.'"

19 The disciples did as Jesus told them to do, and prepared the Passover.

20 Now when the evening had come, He sat down with the twelve.

21 As they were eating, He said, "Truly I say to you that one of you will betray Me."

22 They became very grieved, and all of them began to ask, "Lord, is it I?"

23 He answered, saying, "He that dips his hand with Me in the dish, the same will betray Me.

24 "The Son of Man will go just as it is written of Him, but woe to that man by whom the Son of Man is betrayed! It would have been better for that man if he had not been born."

25 Then Judas, who betrayed him, asked, "Master, is it I?" He said to him, "It is as you have said."

26 As they were eating, Jesus took bread, and blessed it, and broke it, and gave it to the disciples, saying, "Take this and eat it; it is My body."

27 He then took the cup, gave thanks, and gave it to them, saying, "Drink it.

28 "This is My blood of the New Covenant which is shed for many for the remission of their sins.

29 "Now I tell you, I will not drink of this fruit of the vine again until that day when I drink the new with you in My Father's kingdom."

30 When they had sung a hymn, they went out to the Mount of Olives.

31 Then Jesus said to them, "All of you will be offended because of Me tonight: for it is written, **'I will smite the shepherd, and the sheep of the flock shall be scattered abroad'** (Zechariah 13:7).

32 "After I have risen again, I will go before you into Galilee."

33 Peter replied to Him, saying, "Though all men become offended because of You, I will never be offended."

34 Jesus said to him, "Truly I say to you that this very night, before the cock crows, you will deny Me three times."

35 Peter said to Him, "Even if I were to die with You, I will not deny You!" All the disciples said the same.

Gethsemane

36 Then Jesus took the disciples to a place called Gethsemane and said to them, "You sit here while I go over there to pray."

37 So He took with Him Peter and the two sons of Zebedee, and a great heaviness came over Him, and He became very sorrowful.

38 Then He said to them, "My soul is exceedingly sorrowful, even to the point of death. Please stay here, and watch with Me."

39 Then He went a little further and fell on His face, and prayed, saying, "O Father! If it is possible, let this cup pass from Me! Nevertheless, not My will, but Yours be done."

40 When He came to the disciples and found them asleep, He said to Peter, "What? Could you not watch with Me for one hour?

41 "Watch and pray so that you do not enter into temptation. The spirit indeed is willing, but the flesh is weak."

42 He went away again the second time and prayed, saying, "O Father, if this cup may not pass away from Me until I drink it, may Your will be done."

43 Then He came and found them asleep again because their eyes were heavy.

44 So He left them, and went away again, and prayed the third time saying the same thing.

45 When He returned to His disciples He said to them, "Are you sleeping now, taking your rest? The hour is at hand, and the Son of Man will be betrayed into the hands of sinners.

46 "Rise, let us be going. He is close who betrays Me."

Jesus Arrested

47 While He was still speaking, Judas, one of the twelve, came with a great multitude bearing swords and spears, having been sent from the chief priests and elders of the people.

48 Now he who betrayed Him gave them a sign, saying, "Whoever I kiss, that is Him. Arrest Him quickly."

49 So he went directly to Jesus and said, "Hail Master!" and kissed Him.

50 Jesus said to him, "Friend, why have you come?" Then they came and seized Jesus to take Him away.

51 One of the disciples that was with Jesus drew his sword and struck a servant of the high priest, cutting off his ear.

52 Then Jesus said to him, "Put away your sword! They that take up the sword will die by the sword.

53 "Do you not think that I could pray to My Father and He would send Me twelve legions of angels?

54 "How then would the Scriptures be fulfilled that it must happen like this?"

55 Then Jesus said to the multitude, "Have you come out as if to take a thief with swords and spears to take Me? I sat daily with you teaching in the temple, and you did not try to arrest Me.

56 "All of this was done so that the Scriptures of the prophets might be fulfilled." Then all of His disciples forsook Him, and fled.

Trial Before the Sanhedrin

57 They that had laid hold of Jesus led Him away to Caiaphas the high priest, where the scribes and the elders were assembled.

58 Peter followed Him from a distance to the high priest's palace, and he went in and sat with the servants to see the end.

59 Now the chief priests and elders and all the council sought false witnesses against Jesus so they could put Him to death.

60 Though many false witnesses came, yet none condemned Him. At the last, two false witnesses came,

61 and said, "This fellow said, 'I am able to destroy the temple of God and to build it in three days.'"

62 The high priest arose and said to Him, "Do You not answer? What about the thing that these two witnesses just said against You?"

63 Jesus remained silent. The high priest said to Him, "I adjure You by the living God that You tell us whether You are the Christ, the Son of God."

64 Jesus said to him, "It is as you have said. Nevertheless I say to you, after this you will see the Son of Man sitting at the right hand of power and coming in the clouds of heaven."

65 Then the high priest rent his clothes, saying, "He has blasphemed! Why do we have further need of witnesses now that you have heard His blasphemy?

66 "What do you think?" They answered and said, "He is guilty and deserves death."

67 Then they spit in His face and pushed Him, and others struck Him with the palms of their hands,

68 saying, "Prophesy to us, You Christ. Who is it that struck You?"

Peter's Denial

69 Now Peter sat outside in the palace, and a young girl came to him, saying, "You were with Jesus of Galilee."

70 He denied it before them all, saying, "I do not know what you are talking about."

71 When he had gone out onto the porch, another maid saw him and said to them that were there, "This fellow was also with Jesus of Nazareth."

72 Again he denied it with an oath, "I do not know the man."

73 After a while they came to him that were standing around and said to Peter, "Surely you are also one of them. Your speech betrays you."

74 Then he began to curse and to swear, saying, "I do not know the man." Immediately a cock crowed.

75 Peter then remembered the words of Jesus, which He had told him previously, "Before the cock crows, you will deny Me three times." Then he went out and wept bitterly.

Matthew 26:1-5: Jesus had to be crucified on the Passover because He was God's Passover Lamb. Even though the leaders expressed not wanting to do it at the feast, they did anyway, perfectly fulfilling the type without knowing it.

Anointed for Burial

26:6-13: Extravagant worship of Jesus is always appropriate. Her worship would be a memorial to her wherever the gospel is preached. Has our worship been worthy to be remembered?

Betrayal and Denial

26:14-35: Right after the Son of God gave the ritual to celebrate salvation, which we have by the shedding of His own blood and the giving of His body, His closest disciples would betray Him, deny Him, and scatter from Him when He would need His friends the most. Though He had known this was coming, He had still "earnestly desired" to have this last meal with them. Throughout history, His people would make some of the most grievous mistakes and failures, but He would never leave them nor forsake them or deny that they were His. He will never leave us nor forsake us regardless of how much we may fail Him. What kind of God would love those so

much who are such a mess? He is certainly worthy of far more adoration and devotion than He receives. There is no way that we could ever repay Him, but let us resolve to do the best we can for He is worthy.

Gethsemane

26:36-46: In His deepest distress, even His closest friends could not stay awake to stand with Him. Nevertheless, He persevered and went to the cross for their sakes and for us. Knowing how weak and undependable His disciples were, and we would be, He still gave Himself for us. The main thing He asked of us is that we would show grace and mercy to one another. Certainly we can do this for Him.

Jesus Arrested

26:47-56: This is the way that the most righteous nation on earth treated the most righteous Man to ever walk the earth. This is how far we have fallen.

This is the nation whose whole hope was on the coming Messiah, but because He did not come in the manner they were expecting or wanting, this is how He was treated. No nation on earth would have done any better. If this were not a revelation of how far from God we have fallen, His own disciples then fled from Him. We may think that we would not have done this, which is the way that Peter responded, but like him, those who have this pride would have been leading the race to get away. We must take to heart this revelation of how far from Him we are and how much we need to repent and seek Him.

Trial Before the Sanhedrin

26:57-68: The trial of Jesus violated almost every principle of justice in the law, and the consequences for violating these principles are what came upon the Jewish nation.

Peter's Denial

26:69-75: We may, like Peter, think that we will never deny Him, but just having that presumption almost assures that we will. Pride comes before a fall, and such pride that we are better than others will lead us to do the same things. We have probably all denied the Lord because He said as we have done to the least of His little ones we have done unto Him. To the degree that we failed to stand up for any of His people, even the least of them, we failed to stand up for Him.

NOTES

The Gospel of
MATTHEW
Matthew 27

The Price of the Savior

1 When the morning had come, all the chief priests and elders of the people took counsel against Jesus in order to put Him to death.

2 Then they had Him bound and led Him away to be delivered to Pontius Pilate, the governor.

3 When Judas, who had betrayed Him, saw that He had been condemned, he was sorry for what he had done, and brought back the thirty pieces of silver to the chief priests and elders,

4 saying, "I have sinned by betraying innocent blood." They replied, "What is that to us? See to that yourself."

5 He then cast the pieces of silver down in the temple, departed and hung himself.

6 The chief priests took the silver pieces and said, "It is not lawful to put them into the treasury, because it is the price of blood."

7 So they took counsel and bought the potter's field with the money to bury strangers in.

8 Therefore that field was called "The Field of Blood" to this day.

9 By this it was fulfilled that had been spoken by the prophet, saying, **"And they took the thirty pieces of silver, the price of Him that was valued, whom the children of Israel did value;**

10 **"and gave them for the potter's field, as the Lord appointed me"** (Zechariah 11:12-13).

Jesus Before Pilate

11 As Jesus stood before the governor he asked Him, "Are You the King of the Jews?" Jesus replied to him, "It is as you have said."

12 As He was being accused by the chief priests and elders, He did not answer any of their charges.

13 Then Pilate said to Him, "Do You not hear all of these things that they say to bear witness against You?"

14 But He did not answer him a word, which caused the governor to marvel greatly.

15 Now at that feast the governor would release to the people a prisoner whomever they chose,

16 and at that time there was a notable prisoner called Barabbas.

17 So when the people were gathered together, Pilate said to them, "Who do you want me to release to you? Barabbas, or Jesus who is called the Christ?"

18 For he knew that it was because of envy that they had delivered Him to be condemned.

19 When he had sat down on the judgment seat, his wife sent a message to him, saying, "Have nothing to do with that just man, because I have suffered many things this day in a dream because of Him."

20 Even so, the chief priests and elders persuaded the multitude to ask for Barabbas in order to destroy Jesus.

21 The governor answered and said to them, "Which of the two do you want me to release to you?" They said, "Barabbas."

22 Pilate said to them, "What should I do then with Jesus who is called the Christ?" They all said to him, "Let Him be crucified."

23 The governor then asked, "Why? What evil has He done?" So they cried out even more, saying, "Let Him be crucified."

24 When Pilate saw that he could not prevail, but rather that a riot was starting, he took water and washed his hands before the multitude, saying, "I am innocent of the blood of this just man. This is your own doing."

25 Then all of the people answered and said, "His blood be on us, and on our children."

26 Then he released Barabbas to them. After he had Jesus scourged, he delivered Him to be crucified.

Jesus Tortured

27 Then the soldiers of the governor took Jesus into the common hall and gathered the whole band of soldiers around Him,

28 and they stripped Him and put a scarlet robe on Him.

29 Then they made a crown of thorns and put it upon His head, and put a reed in His right hand, and then bowed the knee before Him and mocked Him, saying, "Hail, King of the Jews!"

30 Then they spit on Him and took the reed, and beat Him on the head.

31 After they had mocked Him, they took the robe off of Him, and put His own garments back on Him, and led Him away to be crucified.

32 As they came out they found a man of Cyrene, Simon by name, and compelled him to carry His cross.

33 When they had come to a place called Golgotha, which means, "the place of the skull,"

34 they gave Him vinegar to drink mingled with gall, but when He had tasted it, He would not drink.

Jesus Is Crucified

35 Then they crucified Him, and parted His garments, casting lots for them that it might be fulfilled which was spoken by the prophet, **"They parted My garments among them, and upon My vesture did they cast lots"** (Psalm 22:18).

36 After this they sat down to watch Him,

37 and set over His head where His accusation was written, "THIS IS JESUS THE KING OF THE JEWS."

38 There were also two thieves crucified with Him, one on the right hand and another on the left.

39 All who passed by reviled Him, wagging their heads,

40 saying, "You who would destroy the temple and rebuild it in three days, save Yourself! If You are the Son of God, come down from the cross."

41 Likewise also the chief priests were mocking Him, along with the scribes and elders, saying,

42 "He saved others, but He cannot save Himself. If He is the King of Israel, let Him now come down from the cross, and then we will believe Him.

43 "He trusted in God, so let God deliver Him now if He will have Him, because He said, 'I am the Son of God.'"

44 The thieves also, which were crucified with Him, were casting insults at Him.

45 Then at noon a great darkness came over all of the land until 3:00 p.m.

46 At about 3:00 p.m. Jesus cried with a loud voice, saying, "Eli, Eli, lama sabachthani?" that is to say, "My God, My God! Why have You forsaken Me?"

47 Some who stood there that heard this said, "This man is calling for Elijah."

48 Immediately one of them ran and took a sponge, filled it with vinegar and put it on a reed, and gave Him a drink.

49 The rest said, "Let Him alone. Let us see whether Elijah will come to save Him."

Jesus Yields Up His Life

50 Jesus, when He had cried again with a loud voice, yielded up His Spirit.

51 As He did, immediately the earth quaked and the veil of the temple was rent in two from the top to the bottom, and the rocks were split in two.

52 At the same time, some of the graves were opened, and many of the saints who slept arose;

53 and they came out of the graves after His resurrection and went into the holy city and appeared to many.

54 Now when the centurion and those who were with him watching Jesus saw the earthquake, and these things that were done, a great fear came upon them, and they said, "Truly this was the Son of God!"

55 Many women who followed Jesus from Galilee, serving Him, were there watching from a distance.

56 Among them were Mary Magdalene, and Mary the mother of James and Joseph, and the mother of Zebedee's children.

Jesus Buried

57 When the evening had come, a rich man of Arimathea named Joseph, who was also a disciple of Jesus,

58 went to Pilate and asked for the body of Jesus. Then Pilate commanded that the body be delivered to him.

59 When Joseph had taken the body, he wrapped it in a clean linen cloth,

60 and laid it in his own new tomb, which he had hewn out in the rock. Then he rolled a great stone over the door of the tomb and departed.

61 Mary Magdalene and the other Mary sat against the tomb.

62 Now the next day following the day of the preparation, the chief priests and Pharisees came together to Pilate,

63 saying, "Sir, we remember that this deceiver said while He was still alive, "After three days I will rise again.""

64 Therefore, command that the tomb be made secure until the third day to prevent His disciples from coming by night and stealing Him away, and then saying to the people, "He has risen from the dead." Then the last error will be worse than the first.

65 Pilate said to them, "You have a guard; go and make it as secure as you can."

66 So they went and made the tomb secure, sealing the stone, and setting a watch.

The Price of the Savior

Matthew 27:1-10: From the time in the wilderness when Israel was required to pay a half shekel of silver for their redemption, silver has been a symbol of redemption. Jesus, the Lord of glory, was valued at just thirty pieces of silver.

Many historians and scholars believed that Judas never intended for Jesus to be harmed or executed, but rather that by betraying Him, he would force Jesus to take His authority as the King of Israel. Perhaps, but when you have an opening in your heart for the devil to enter as Judas did, you will find yourself able to justify almost any evil thing, but the consequences are still evil. Jesus, the King of kings, would never take His authority because of the manipulation of men, even His own followers.

Jesus Before Pilate

27:11-26: That the entire multitude demanded that Jesus be crucified was a fulfillment of the prophecy of the Passover Lamb when the whole nation of Israel was commanded to kill it at twilight.

This was the same multitude who had just five days before cried, "Hosanna! Blessed is He who comes in the name of the Lord," when Jesus entered the city. This reveals how unstable any mob can be. No lover of the truth will follow a mob but will follow the truth as it is revealed to them.

Jesus Tortured

27:27-34: The King of glory, the Creator of the universe, suffered this humiliation because He loves us that much. He did this for those who were mocking and beating Him. This is the love of God that the whole creation will marvel at forever.

This also reveals the depravity of man when the most righteous nation on earth would do this to the most just, righteous One who ever walked the earth. This is why we need the Savior, and the atonement that He made for us.

Vinegar and gall were sometimes given to those being executed to deaden the pain. Jesus refused this in order to pay the full price for us.

Jesus Is Crucified

27:35-49: Men still mock Jesus by mocking and ridiculing His followers, but the day will come when every knee will bow to Him, and they will mourn for Him. However, He is not coming back to retaliate. He did not go to the cross to get revenge, but so that He could save even those who would so mistreat Him and His people. We must maintain the same love even for our enemies because He paid this price for them too.

Jesus Yields Up His Life

27:50-56: In Genesis, much is devoted to Abraham finding a burial place for his wife Sarah. He also chose to be buried there, as did Isaac, Jacob, and Joseph. Joseph was even listed among the great heroes of the faith for making Israel swear to carry his bones and bury him there when they would be delivered from Egypt. The place of their burial was Hebron, just south of Jerusalem. This is why they were so insistent on this place—as Jesus put it, they had "seen His day," and they wanted to be a part of it as the first resurrection after the cross. These are the saints who rose on this day.

Jesus Buried

27:57-66: There was no amount of force that man could have provided to prevent the resurrection of Christ. Whether four guards, or an army of guards, the outcome would have still been the same.

NOTES

THE GOSPEL OF
MATTHEW
Matthew 28

Jesus Rises From the Dead

1 At the end of the Sabbath, as it began to dawn toward the first day of the week, Mary Magdalene and the other Mary came to see the tomb.

2 There was a great earthquake, because the angel of the Lord descended from heaven and came and rolled back the stone from the door, and then sat on it.

3 His countenance was like lightning, and his clothing was as white as snow.

4 Because of their fear of him, the guards shook and fell to the ground like dead men.

5 This angel said to the women, "Do not fear, because I know that you seek Jesus who was crucified.

6 "He is not here because He has arisen just as He said. Come and see the place where the Lord was laid.

7 "Now go quickly and tell His disciples that He has risen from the dead, and He will go before you into Galilee. There you will see Him just as you have been told."

8 So they departed quickly from the tomb with fear and great joy, and ran to bring His disciples the word.

9 As they went to tell His disciples, Jesus met them, saying, "Greetings." So they came and held Him by the feet and worshiped Him.

10 Then Jesus said to them, "Do not be afraid. Go tell My brethren that they must go into Galilee, and there they will see Me."

The Plot of the Chief Priests

11 Now those who were on the watch came into the city and showed to the chief priests all that was done.

12 When they were assembled with the elders and had taken counsel, they gave a large sum of money to the soldiers,

13 and said to them, "Say, 'His disciples came by night and stole Him away while we slept.'

14 "If this comes to the governor's ears, we will persuade him not to punish you."

15 So they took the money and did as they were told, and this is the story commonly reported among the Jews until this day.

The Great Commission

16 Then the eleven disciples went away into Galilee, into the mountain where Jesus had directed them.

17 When they saw Him, they worshiped Him, but some doubted.

18 So Jesus came and spoke to them, saying, "All authority has been given to Me in heaven and in earth.

19 "Go therefore, and make disciples of all nations, baptizing them in the name of the Father, the Son, and the Holy Spirit,

20 "teaching them to observe everything that I have commanded you, and I will be with you always, even to the end of the age." Amen.

Jesus Rises From the Dead

Matthew 28:1-10: The greatest hope and the foundation of Christianity is that Jesus rose in ultimate victory over death, and that He will also raise His followers from the dead to live with Him forever. The continued proof of His resurrection is the way He continues to move among His people and through them the work that He began when He walked the earth.

The Plot of the Chief Priests

28:11-15: The proof that Jesus rose from the dead is abundant and continuous, but hard hearts will reject it regardless

of the evidence. No one can come to the Son unless the Father draws them by His Holy Spirit, and even then they must want to know the truth.

The Great Commission

28:16-20: This is the purpose of every Christian: to make disciples of Christ. A disciple is much more than just a convert— a disciple is a student of a master. This is our daily calling—to learn of Him and to lead others to Him to be His disciples also.

Recent studies have shown that less than 10 percent of those who call themselves born-again Christians have a biblical worldview. Those who are true disciples will view the world from Christ's perspective, which few of those who claim to be His actually do. This is evidence that we have been making converts but not disciples. A disciple of Christ was defined by the Lord Himself and was also devoted to knowing all that He commanded. Are we a true disciple?

Just the fact that you have read something like this is a good indication that you are at least seeking to be a true disciple. Let us make this the chief devotion of our lives, as He is worthy to have such devotion who has given so much to us.

NOTES

Book of Matthew
Proper Names and Definitions

Abel: vanity, breath, vapor, a city, mourning, a meadow

Abijah: the Lord is my father

Abiud: father of praise

Abraham: father of a great multitude, exalted father

Achim: preparing, revenging, confirming

Ahaz: one that takes or possesses

Alphaeus: leader or chief

Amminadab: my people are noble

Amon: faithful, true

Andrew: a strong man, manly

Archelaus: the prince of the people

Arimathaea: height

Asa: physician, cure

Azor: a helper, a court

Babylon: confusion, also the gate of god, mixture

Barabbas: son of the father, son of shame, confusion

Barachias: that bows before God

Bartholomew: son of Tolmai, a son that suspends the waters

Beelzebub: god of dung, god of flies

Bethany: the house of song, the house of affliction, place of unripe figs

Bethlehem: house of bread

Bethphage: house of my month, or of early figs

Bethsaida: house of fruits, or of food, or of snares, or of fishing

Boaz: or Booz, in strength

Caesar: title of Roman Emperors

Canaan: merchant, trader, or that humbles and subdues

Canaanite: descendant of Canaan merchant, trader, or that humbles and subdues

Capernaum: the field of repentance, city of comfort, walled village

Chorazin: the secret, here is a mystery

Christ: anointed

Cyrene: a wall, coldness, the floor

Daniel: judgment of God, God my judge

David: well-beloved, dear

Decapolis: containing ten cities

Egypt: the two lands, double straights, that troubles or oppresses, anguish

Eli: the offering or lifting up, God is high

Eliakim: resurrection of God, God is setting up

Elijah: heifer, chariot, round, Yah is God

Eliud: God is my praise

Emmanuel: God with us

Frankincense: pure, to be white

Gadarenes: men of Gadara, i.e., a place surrounded or walled

Galilee: wheel, revolution, circle or circuit

Gehenna: a literal valley outside of Jerusalem where garbage was burned

Gennesaret: garden of the prince, of riches

Gentiles: the nations or pagans

Gethsemane: a very fat or plentiful vale

Golgotha: a heap of skulls, something skull-shaped

Gomorrah: rebellious people, submersion, to deal tyrannically; make merchandise of; a ruined heap

Hen: grace, quiet, rest, favor

Herod: son of a hero, heroic

Hezekiah: strength of the Lord

Hezron: the dart of joy, the division of the song, enclosure

Hosanna: save I pray thee, keep, preserve

Isaac: laughter, he shall laugh, mockery

Isaiah: the salvation of the Lord

Iscariot: man of Kerioth, a man of murder, a hireling

Israel: who prevails with God, he shall be prince of God

Jacob: that supplants, undermines, heel-catcher

James: that supplants, undermines, heel-catcher, he whom God protects

Jeconiah: preparation, or stability, of the Lord

Jehoshaphat: the Lord is judge

Jeremiah: exaltation of the Lord

Jericho: his moon, his month, his sweet smell

Jerusalem: city of peace, vision of peace, foundation of peace, restoring or teaching of peace

Jesse: gift, oblation, one who is, possessor, wealthy, Yahweh exists, man, manly, strong

Jesus: Savior, Deliverer, Yahweh is salvation

John: the grace or mercy of the Lord

Jonah: or Jonas, a dove, he that oppresses, destroyer

Joram: to cast, elevated, Jehovah is exalted

Jordan: the river of judgment, flowing downward, to bring down

Joseph: increase, addition, may God add

Josiah: the Lord burns, the fire of the Lord, healed, supported by Jehovah

Jotham: the perfection of the Lord

Judaea: the praise of the Lord, confession

Judah: the praise of the Lord, confession

Judas: the praise of the Lord, confession

Judea: the praise of the Lord, confession

Lot: wrapped up, hidden, covered, myrrh, rosi

Magadan: tower, greatness

Magdalene: a person from Magdala, tower

Manasseh: forgetfulness, he that is forgotten

Mary: bitterness, rebellion

Matthew: given, a reward, gift of Jehovah

Messiah: anointed

Moses: taken out, drawn forth

Myrrh: bitter, symbolic of the graces of the Messiah

Nahshon: that foretells, that conjectures

Naphtali: that struggles or fights

Nazarene: separated, crowned, sanctified, watchtower

Nazareth: separated, crowned, sanctified, watchtower

Nineveh: handsome, agreeable, abode of Ninus

Noah: repose, consolation, that quavers or totters Zelophehad's daughter

Obed: a servant, workman, worshiper

Passover: to pass or to spring over, to spare

Perez: breakthrough, breach, divided

Peter: a rock or stone

Pharisees: set apart

Philip: warlike, a lover of horses

Phylacteries: things to be especially observed

Pilate: armed with a dart, cap of freedom

Pontius: marine, belonging to the sea

Rabbi: my teacher

Rachel: sheep, ewe, lamb

Rahab: large, extended name of a woman, proud, quarrelsome applied to Egypt, storm, act stormily, boisterous, arrogant, sea monster, strength, broad/breadth

Ram: elevated, sublime

Rehoboam: who sets the people at liberty, the people multiplied

Ruth: drunk, satisfied

Sadducees: followers of Sadoc or Zadok, righteous

Salmon: peaceable, perfect, he that rewards

Samaritans: inhabitants of Samaria

Satan: contrary, adversary, enemy, accuser, deceiver

Shealtiel: asked or lent of God

Sidon: hunting, fishing, venison

Simon: that hears, that obeys

Sodom: their secret, their cement, fettered, scorch, burnt

Solomon: peaceable, perfect, one who recompenses

Syria: Aram, exalted, high tableland

Tamar: palm, palm-tree

Tetrarch: governor of a fourth part

Thomas: a twin

Tyre: Tyrus, strength, rock, sharp

Uriah: or Urijah, the Lord is my light or fire

Uzziah: Uzziel, the strength, or kid, of the Lord

Zacharias: God has remembered

Zadok: just, justified, righteous

Zebedee: abundant, portion, gift of God

Zebulun: Zebulon, dwelling, habitation

Zerah: east, brightness, a rising

Zerubbabel: a stranger at Babylon, dispersion of confusion

Zion: monument, raised up, sepulcher, fortification, permanent capital, barren, dry, desert